T0365364

THE FINAL HOURS OF DARKNESS

Keith Grossl

AuthorHouse™ LLC
1663 Liberty Drive
Bloomington, IN 47403
www.authorhouse.com
Phone: 1-800-839-8640

Published by AuthorHouse 6/3/2014

ISBN: 978-1-4969-1675-4(sc)
ISBN: 978-1-4969-1676-1 (e)

authorHOUSE®

Contents

PREFACE

In the predawn hours of an autumn night, a young boy lay silent beneath trembling sheets. The silver sheen of October's moon provides the only light as he lies there, watchful and afraid. As if only to torment him further, a sudden gust of wind shakes the tree outside his window, giving life to the shadows that now dance across the room, and icy fingers caress his flesh as goose bumps begin to crawl. *It will happen again tonight*, he thinks, *just like it always does.* Then without warning, the imposing clouds of a gathering storm blanket the moon, leaving him vulnerable to the darkness that surrounds him. His heart pounds as he listens for the chilling sounds of a nightmare come to call, but when his breath turns to frozen mist, he knows he's not alone. He's back! The shadow man is back!

Gripping his pillow tightly, he warns himself, *Don't fall asleep, don't even close your eyes!* But they grow heavy as he struggles to stay alert, waiting for the final hours of darkness when the light of day will come and rid him of the fear and that which he knows is real!

INTRODUCTION

One of my fondest memories of childhood was sitting up late on a Saturday night watching those old, black-and-white horror movies. I can still hear the dramatic music they played as the webbed claw of Gillman reached up from the murky depths and grabbed the side of the boat. Or the foreboding fog that rolled through the woods as the wolf man stalked his latest victim.

But every movie I watched lacked one vital element—reality. Even as a young boy, I knew such things weren't real, and if Godzilla ever crawled up out of the briny deep and ate Tokyo, it would be all over the news. But there was one thing that did ring true for me, and that was the stories my parents would tell. On occasion they would reminisce about a house in West Virginia and the unusual sounds that could be heard in the night. My mother shuddered as she recalled a time when she was alone in the house but could hear the heavy footfalls of a man on the stairs.

When the sound reached the top of the stairs, it turned and came down the hall toward her room, where it stopped, as if knowing exactly where to find her. "In the dark, I couldn't see the door knob," she said, "but I could hear it slowly turning, and I knew someone was out there in the hallway. I was just about to scream when suddenly whoever or whatever was out there began to fade away." Both my parents claimed to have heard the sound of a baby crying late at night, even though there was never any baby in the house.

Such stories went on and on. Even the neighbors were aware of the paranormal activity that occurred there, and one man who would drive past every morning on his way to work suddenly began driving nearly three miles out of his way just to avoid it. He said he saw something in the front yard one night while on his way home, and though he never told anyone what it was he had seen, no one ever knew him to go near the house again.

I never doubted the honesty of their stories; in fact, I sometimes wondered why such things shouldn't be real. It took nothing more than a glance in the mirror for me to see the spark of life behind my own eyes, and I wondered why its light would be extinguished in death.

Then one Saturday night I found a movie of great interest; it was the original 1963 version of *The Haunting*. With a bath towel blocking out the light from under the door so my parents wouldn't know I was still awake, I turned down the lights and watched as the silhouette of an old mansion filled the TV screen. The narrator described its age. It was the kind of house people called haunted, he said, but now silence lay steadily against the wood and stone of

Hillhouse, and whatever walked there walked alone! Goose bumps crawled up my arms as I watched.

The movie was like an echo of the stories I had grown up with—unexplained sounds, cold spots, locked doors found open, and locals who won't come near. The movie seemed to confirm every story I had ever heard, and as I lay there on my bed with the lights down low, the seeds of curiosity began to sprout.

Soon I began looking for stories of the paranormal anywhere I could find them. But a feeling of skepticism began to develop when similarity and coincidence made their appearance. All too often, a story will open with a family finding the house of their dreams, a house large enough to accommodate the entire family and usually located near work and school. Naturally the house is priced to fit their meager budget, and it soon begins to look as if they were lured into some kind of trap. Without warning, their dream house will then turn into a nightmare as the demonic forces haunting it make themselves known.

With nowhere else to turn, the frightened family begins asking neighbors if they have any explanation for the strange things that have been happening. And with a genuine look of concern, their neighbors will fill them in on the terrifying history of the house. Suddenly, everything begins to make sense.

I know that some of these stories may have been dressed up a bit in order to make them more interesting and certainly scarier. But where does the truth end and the fabrication begin? Other stories of the paranormal were nothing more than secondhand accounts, accounts that left the details blurry and the facts amiss. When I thought back to the stories my parents told, I believed them then, and I believe them now. But I also know that even the most honest and trusted people can be mistaken, while others eager for attention will say anything, and I began to realize that without proof or at least some kind of evidence, all stories are nothing more than that—stories. The taste of reality is sometimes bitter, but in my search for the truth, I began to see that nothing I would ever read or see in a movie could equal having the experience myself.

While I was still just a boy, I could do little more than continue reading books and watching movies, but as an adult, I finally had my own personal experience. It was both terrifying and amazing, but more importantly, it was the evidence I had been looking for, and now my beliefs were set in stone. Years later, with my feelings of skepticism diminished, I sat flipping through a magazine where I found an article that told of a house in Pennsylvania, a house that was said to be haunted, and from there my quest into the world of the paranormal began.

CHAPTER ONE

SOMEONE'S AT THE DOOR

My Personal Experience

A few weeks before Jayne and I were to be married, we found an apartment in the city. It certainly wasn't "the perfect home," as in most of the ghost stories I've read; in fact, it was a rather ordinary place. I moved in, bringing all the furniture we needed for the kitchen and living room. The bedroom needed something more suitable for two, so we decided to purchase new furnishings. Until then, I placed a mattress in one corner of the room and discarded most everything else I had.

The room had no overhead light or switches on any of the walls, so I put a small desk lamp on the floor beside me. With it was my clock radio and an unloaded revolver that once belonged to my father. I never felt the need to purchase bullets or keep the gun loaded, but knowing I could gave me a small sense of security. For now, I simply kept it on the floor beside me.

My first night in the apartment was uneventful; it was the second night when my story began to unfold. I had gone to bed early, but sleep became restless as the night went on. In a dream, the figure of a woman stood watching me from the foot of my bed. Clad in a black robe, she kept the hood pulled down, concealing her face and anything else about her that might have seemed human.

Like something that had emerged from the darkest corners of the nether world, she stood there staring at me, faceless and cold, the ominous shadow of someone who had once belonged in our world. Though she never spoke or tried to communicate, what she represented was clear; she, or rather it, was a creature of jealousy and hate. As the hooded figure stood watching me from the foot of the bed, it began to drift slowly toward the opposite side of the room. Passing through the closed bedroom door, it never once turned around or took its eyes off of me. I sat up in bed, eyes wide as I searched the room, but the figure in black was gone. I began to relax, realizing it had only been a dream and that no one was ever there at all. Feeling calmer now, I thought out loud, "I'm glad it was only a dream." But then as if in response, the bedroom door began to rattle. Violently it shook back and forth like someone trying frantically to escape a locked room, or someone enraged and trying to get in! All thoughts of the woman in black vanished as a jolt of reality shook me wide awake. *Someone has gotten into the apartment*, was my only thought, and in my panic, I searched desperately for something I could use as a weapon but found only the empty revolver.

The darkness would make it impossible to tell the gun wasn't loaded, and my threat would seem real. But still the gun that once gave me a sense of security could now only provide a feeling of helplessness as I watched the door rattle and bang in its frame. Sitting there alone in the darkness with only an unloaded pistol between me and the intruder, a more startling realization came to mind: the door had no lock! With nothing to prevent the intruder from entering the room, I braced myself for what I knew would happen next. Any second the door would burst open, and I would be face to face with the intruder, armed with nothing more than a bluff. I waited. Then just as suddenly as it began, the door stopped rattling, but it never burst open, and no one ever came in. I sat there listening intently for any sound at all, but the apartment was still and quiet, and in the silence that followed, I had an opportunity to wonder who it was that stood on the other side of the door and what it might be that prevented him from opening it. But the harder I tried to make sense of what was happening, the more confusing it all became. By rattling the door, the intruder had announced his presence, giving me a chance to respond.

If there had been a phone line in the room with me, I may have already called the police, not to mention the gun in my hand. Had I ever felt the need to keep it loaded, my reaction may have been deadly, yet he was clearly unafraid of what my response might be. Sitting there alone in the bedroom, listening for even the slightest sound, it seemed more and more likely that no one had been in the apartment other than me. But what could have caused the door to rattle so violently? I tried to think of a logical explanation to answer that question, but I was completely baffled. I continued to wait and listen until I felt certain I was alone. I put the gun down on the floor, thinking out loud as I did, "Well, whatever it was it's over now." Then just as suddenly as before, the door again began to rattle. But this time it was as if it wanted me to know, *I can hear you, and I'm still here!*

With the gun back in my hand, I waited until the rattling stopped and the apartment became quiet again. It seemed I should go out and try to find an explanation for what had just happened, but a voice from somewhere deep inside warned me, *Don't open that door!* By this time, I wasn't sure anyone else was in the apartment, but I was sure doors didn't rattle themselves.

Sometimes even now I wonder what I may have encountered had I gotten up and opened the door. But whatever it was it was gone now, and with it went all sense of fear.

A feeling of wonder was all that remained of those very frightening few minutes, but I didn't stay up much longer trying to think of an explanation. There would be plenty of time for that tomorrow.

My eyes shot open that morning to the sound of my alarm clock chirping loudly. It announced the beginning of a new day, and I lay there for only a moment before reaching over and slapping it quiet. It was just as any other morning had ever been. I had no thoughts of the paranormal or any dark figure watching me from the shadows; my only concern was getting ready for work. I pulled myself up off of the mattress and left the bedroom. Stepping into the living room, my eyes locked on the front door and the small chain that hung in front of it. The memory of what happened last night flooded my mind as I realized no one could have gotten in without breaking the chain, but everything in the living room was as it should have been. Nothing of value was missing, and nothing had been moved. Before going into the kitchen to make coffee, I imagined the sight of broken glass all over the floor where someone had gotten in through the window, but nothing was out of the ordinary. The windows were shut and locked just as they had been when I first moved in.

After starting a pot of coffee, I walked back down the hall, stopping at the open bedroom door. I peeked in and found my revolver on the floor exactly where I remembered leaving it. Clearly what had happened last night was not a dream, but after checking the front door and every window in the apartment, it was also clear that no one had gotten in during the night. For now, there was little else I could do but put the mystery behind me and get ready for work.

Over the next few days, I also noticed something strange about the basement laundry room; it seemed occupied. Even though I was certain no one was down there with me, I had the distinct impression I wasn't alone. I don't claim to be psychic, but I could feel the presence of about half a dozen people standing around watching me. The feeling wasn't malevolent or threatening in any way; it seemed more as if they were waiting for something and watching me out of boredom. Like people standing at a bus stop watching the traffic go by, I simply attracted their attention.

When Jayne moved in, I thought it would be for the best if I didn't tell her about my experience in the bedroom or how I felt in the basement. It all seemed too incredible to talk about, and I couldn't be sure what her reaction might be. After all, she would have to sleep in that same bedroom, and the laundry room was a convenience I didn't want to frighten her away from.

However, as the next few days turned into weeks, it became apparent that Jayne had also felt something in the basement, something that made her feel uneasy. With a basket full of laundry, she marched dutifully out to the car, and then off she went. Every time and without fail, I would see her do this, walking across the courtyard to the parking lot where she would load the car with laundry, sometimes making two trips before driving more than a mile to the Laundromat. Having few other tenants in our building left the laundry room open most of the time, but Jayne didn't seem to care much for the convenience, and I didn't need to ask her why. Still, I felt there might be some logical reason for her actions, but when asked, she would only shrug her shoulders and say, "I guess I just like the Laundromat better."

Months had gone by before I told her about my experience in the bedroom. Her eyes widened as I did, and she looked at me with an uneasy interest. "I never felt anything strange or frightening in our apartment," she said. "It's the basement that bothers me. It's like there are people down there, and they watch me!"

Chills ran down my spine. "You feel it too?"

She nodded. "Yeah, I feel it too."

Our experiences were both frightening and fascinating, but when spring had turned to summer that year with no further disturbances, I all but forgot about that second night in the apartment. Jayne also seemed happy, though she continued to avoid the basement.

Saturday was warm and sunny, and the paranormal events that had occurred were now nothing more than a curious memory. Jayne had gone out that afternoon, and I had nothing more to do than flip from channel to channel searching for something to watch on television. I sat there on the couch feeling hopelessly bored when I noticed the amount of dishes that had begun to pile up in the kitchen sink.

This wasn't the time most people would think of dark and frightening things, but I couldn't help remembering that second night in the apartment and how the bedroom door shook and rattled by itself. I used a dish towel to wipe the warm, soapy water from my hands and forearms as I walked down the hall to the bedroom. I already knew the door was firmly hung in its frame, but out of disbelief, I had to try it again. Grabbing hold of the door knob, I pulled and pushed back and forth as fast and hard as I could, but the door wouldn't budge.

This only added one more question to the puzzle: how did the door rattle that night if I couldn't even do it deliberately? I went back to the kitchen and returned to the task of washing dishes. Standing in front of the kitchen sink, I tried to make sense of what happened that night, but the harder I tried, the more impossible it seemed to be. I even began to wonder how ridiculous it would be to just except the possibility of a ghost.

There isn't much to fear from things that go bump in the night, not on a sunny Saturday afternoon, and curiosity made me feel even less afraid. I thought a lot about that night the bedroom door rattled and the feeling of people in the basement laundry room, but right now I felt that—more than anything—I just needed to know what really happened. It seemed a bit foolish at first, but as I looked around the room, I spoke out loud to the atmosphere around me. "Can you hear me?" I asked. "Do something to prove you're real. Show yourself," I said, but nothing happened, and I can't say I really thought anything would. *I'm sure making contact with the dead is a little more complicated than that,* I thought, so a little disappointed and somewhat amused with myself, I stepped into the living room for a cigarette. As I did, I heard the sound of something crash to the floor behind me. Startled, I turned around to find a coffee cup broken on the floor. Strangely, the cup was in the middle of the floor, nowhere near the countertop or the kitchen table, making it impossible for the cup to have simply toppled over the edge and land where it did. It had to have been picked up and dropped there.

As I cleaned up the broken glass, I discovered something else, something more disturbing. The cup that had broken was the only cup we owned that had my name printed on it. Now even on a sunny Saturday afternoon, I felt I had something to be afraid of. *It knows my name!*

That following week, I felt both curious and a little uneasy. It was hard for me to believe any of this was really happening, but it was, and when the coffee cup crashed to the floor behind me, I knew it was in response to the things I had said, just as if it wanted me to know, *I am real, and I'm standing right next to you!* I tried to put it out of my mind, and as the week continued, I had all but forgotten about it. But by ten o'clock Saturday evening, only one week after my experience in the kitchen, I would be reminded once again that Jayne and I weren't alone in the apartment. We were at home that evening relaxing in front of the television. Jayne was sitting in a recliner across the room from me. From where she sat, she was able to see partway down the hall just past our bedroom door. I turned down the volume of the television when we began talking about buying a home of our own, but in midsentence, a sudden look of startled surprise crossed her face.

"There's someone in our house!" she shouted, jumping to her feet. As she dashed across the living room toward our bedroom, I had already gotten up.

"What are you talking about?" I asked. But she didn't answer me; she only disappeared into the darkened room. I tried to explain to her that our windows were at least ten feet from the ground outside and that no one could have gotten in without at least being heard, but when she stepped back into the hallway, her eyes were wide and frightened.

"He's in the bathroom," was all she said.

When we went into the bathroom, I showed her something I already knew; the bathroom window was very small and painted shut. "No one could have gotten in or out," I said.

Jayne could only stare blankly at the window and then back at me. Then she described how she had seen a boy of about eleven or twelve walk out of our bedroom and then down the hall toward the bathroom. She seemed to have trouble describing him in detail and was a bit confused by what she had just seen. "He had a burgundy robe with gray trim," she said, "but as quickly as I had seen him, he was gone." I had no doubt in the truth of what she was saying. She was frightened and very puzzled. We went back into the living room and sat down as she tried to explain that she really did see a boy in the hallway.

I remembered that Saturday afternoon when the coffee cup crashed to the floor behind me and what I had said. The first thing I had asked was, "Can you hear me?" Then I asked it to do something that would prove to me it was real, but the last thing I said was, "Show yourself!" I didn't know if he had chosen to reveal himself to my wife or if she caught him off guard and only glimpsed him by mistake, but soon we would share the experience.

On Wednesday morning a few days later, I woke up for work a little earlier than usual. The room was dark, and Jayne lay sleeping beside me. I made sure not to wake her as I got out of bed and made my way out of the room. Except for the dim glow cast by outside lights shining through the kitchen windows, the rest of the apartment was just as dark, but as I stepped into the living room, I saw him for myself. A boy of about twelve years old drifted along a dim and misty pathway of light from the kitchen to the middle of the living room. I had barely enough time for my mind to put the pieces together and understand what I was seeing when suddenly he was gone. I don't remember the color of his robe or the gray trim Jayne had described, only that he was solid from head to shoulders but became increasingly translucent until he was invisible from just below his knees. The boy was shrouded in a misty haze as he drifted across the darkened room, completely unaware of me as I stood there watching him, and then he was gone.

I never saw the phantom boy again after that, the bedroom door didn't rattle any more, and there were no other unexplainable events.

As summer came to an end that year, Jayne and I found the house we had been looking for, and we left the apartment with its mysteries unsolved.

Chapter Two

Night Sounds

Some Experience Preferred

As Jayne and I approached the Farnsworth House on Baltimore Street in Gettysburg, Pennsylvania, for the first time, it was plain to see that something made it stand out from all the rest. The sturdy, two-story brick home seemed filled to capacity with its memories of all the many years gone by and every life spent there, both lived and lost.

There a gentle-handed midwife cared for a young mother in labor, a father grieved over the loss of his beloved son, and three Confederate sharpshooters fought their final battle from the attic window above.

The brick portion of the house, which was built in 1833, was what I was primarily concerned with and was definitely one of the more historic structures in town. In July of 1863, Confederate soldiers marched into town, pushing Union troops out, taking possession of Gettysburg. Ejected Union forces, however, took up new positions in the cemetery, and the Battle of Gettysburg began.

Using the surrounding structures to their advantage, the Confederate Army placed sharpshooters in strategic areas, such as the attic window of the Farnsworth House. Hurriedly, the men placed there began pushing furniture against the walls in hopes of blocking out the large-caliber bullets being fired at them from the cemetery. Caught in the crossfire was young Mary Virginia Wade, taking a Union stand the only way she could, by baking bread to feed hungry Union troops. However, by the end of the three-day conflict, Ginnie Wade lay dead on the floor, killed by a single shot possibly fired from the Farnsworth House.

The three Confederate sharpshooters positioned at the attic window had also been killed in what must have seemed a true hailstorm of lead. Today more than one hundred bullet holes can still be seen on that side of the house, bullet holes that bear witness to the courage and sacrifice of the people who were there those three days in July of 1863.

But perhaps something more than physical evidence remains. Perhaps the atmosphere of the attic has been stained by the great expenditures of emotions that must have occurred during the battle.

More than one hundred years later, many people believe that the duty-bound souls of those three soldiers still remain in the attic, holding their positions against the Union Army. Heavy boots walking back and forth, furniture being moved, and the sound of a mouth harp can still be heard coming from the attic above.

Only a few steps down and around the corner is the Catherine Sweeney Room. Unlike the attic above, it's comfortable and attractive. The bright floral wallpaper and antique furniture are certainly eye catching and decorative, but this room also holds its own memories of people and the tragic events that shaped their lives.

Mary, a midwife during the 1800s, hurries to the bedside of a young woman in labor. Sadly, the fragile life within her cannot be saved, and she will never come to know the baby she has dreamed of. It was here in the Catherine Sweeney Room that her hopes and dreams of motherhood were lost forever, and now her sorrow echoes through time. Even men are sometimes brought to tears as they are overcome by an inexplicable feeling of loss. Just as the attic has been stained by the expenditure of emotions in battle, this room also seems to hold within its walls a young mother's broken heart. And the sound that Mary's floor-length dress made as she rushed to her bedside can still be heard in the night.

Next door to the Catherine Sweeney Room is the Sarah Black Room. Although equally comfortable and attractive, this room bears instead the shadow of a father's broken heart. The room was once used by Mary as a bedroom, and in the days before indoor plumbing, the oversized bathroom was a nursery where she kept and cared for the newborn children of Gettysburg. But somewhere in the hallway just outside remains a memory of pain and sorrow that haunts the living even today.

Here in this bedroom, a five-year-old boy's broken body lay still and quiet, his laughter trampled into a silence his father's heart simply cannot bear. Was it the carelessness of a small boy at play or the taunting and teasing of older boys that sent Jeremy dashing into the traffic on Baltimore Street? Only one thing is certain, and that's the horror his father must have felt as his son fell beneath the crushing wheels of the oncoming horse and carriage. Jeremy, broken and bleeding, was brought into the Farnsworth House and laid out in the Sarah Black Room. With no doctor in town, Mary was the only one they could turn to, but the 1800s midwife could do little to help, and within a few hours, Jeremy was lost forever.

It's believed that his father still bears the pain and sorrow of that terrible day and on some nights can be heard pacing just outside in the hallway, where he waits for word of his son's condition. Also, a photograph taken in the Sarah Black Room shows a smoky apparition standing at the foot of the bed. It's believed by some to be the ghost of Jeremy's father saying good-bye to his son for the last time.

On other nights, people say they have heard the sound of a small boy running up and down that same hallway, laughing and playing just as any other child would. Suddenly the toilet may flush, or very often the sound of someone banging on the steam pipes can be plainly heard.

This was just the type of place where I had always dreamed of staying, so when Jayne and I were shown to our room, the Catherine Sweeney Room, I was filled with excitement at the prospects of spending the night in a house that is known to be haunted.

In the apartment that Jayne and I shared years before, we had several strange experiences, but without any known history of paranormal activity or even one rumor of a haunted past, every event was numbed by astonishment and disbelief. Hopefully tonight I would be able to experience the full impact of a haunting by knowing what was happening as it happened.

And perhaps in this way I would be able to grasp the reality of it and in some way reach out and touch the next world.

We had just begun unpacking the simple equipment we brought with us when, remembering film she left behind, Jayne went back out to the car, leaving me alone for the moment. I sat down on the edge of the bed and tried to get a feel for the room and its unseen occupants.

I somehow felt as though I had stepped from the world of today into a world that contained all the sentiment of yesterday, but none of it was clear to me. The room held its cards close, refusing to reveal its secrets. I had no sense of a mother's loss or the concern of the midwife trying desperately to help her. Maybe the feeling of energy I had was only imagination and wishful thinking. Soon even my sense of history began to fade with the sound of traffic and the voices of tourists outside.

I sat alone in the room waiting for Jayne to return when, from the corner of my eye, I glimpsed the silhouette of someone watching me from the bathroom doorway. Just then I heard the sound of Jayne's key in the lock, and as I turned to see her opening the door, the dark figure was already gone. I could only believe it was nothing more than my imagination. After all, I hadn't come this far to jump at shadows; I was here to experience the full impact of a real haunting.

I put the incident out of my mind as Jayne walked across the room at an excited pace. "I think we should hit the battlefield first," she said, dropping new rolls of film on the bed. "It'll be easier to find the places we want to investigate in the daylight, and then we can go back tonight. Maybe until then we could visit a couple of souvenir shops," she said, smiling.

Conveniently, the Farnsworth House has its own parking lot and is within walking distance of most shops. So why not take a walk around town? And with that, we were on our way.

It was nearly eleven o'clock when Jayne and I returned to our room. The sound of tourists had died down, and even the traffic outside had become quiet. Now that the bright afternoon sun was down, the room was dark, revealing a more sinister atmosphere. This time there would be no mistaking the energy I felt for wishful thinking or imagination. The feeling that someone or something was in the room with us was undeniable. The room itself seemed to watch us, whispering its secrets in a language known only to those who dwell in the threshold between what is and what once was.

Jayne and I lay there together in the darkness feeling alert and energized by the atmosphere of the room. Suddenly a sound like a dull thud was heard at the foot of the bed, a sound I had no explanation for. We listened intently for any other sound that would reveal its origin, but no other sound was heard. Although the noise came from only a few feet away, it was easy enough to explain as coming from the Sarah Black Room next door and probably not at all paranormal. But soon another sound broke the silence, the sound of cannon fire.

Four explosions could be heard far off in the distance. However, an explanation for this was easy to find; it was probably nothing more than fireworks left over from the Fourth of July. I was beginning to feel disappointed. I had come all this way, and it seemed nothing would ever happen. Then a new sound broke the silence; it was the sound of someone banging on a metal pipe. The sound seemed to come from every direction, and then it slowly faded away. I couldn't imagine who would bang on a pipe in the middle of the night, but it wasn't the chain-rattling ghost I was looking for. It was merely an unexplained sound. Suddenly Jayne's body jolted like an electric shock had run through her. "Did you hear that?" she said. "Someone's in the bathroom!"

I sat up on one elbow and tried to listen as closely as I could. "Can't you hear that?" she asked. But still I couldn't hear anything. "It's the midwife," Jayne said, her voice sounding a little more frightened than before. "She's in the room with us!" Her body became rigid, and her voice was filled with fear. "My God, she's standing next to me!"

I could only lay there confused by what wasn't happening. I couldn't see or hear anything, and yet my wife was experiencing something extraordinary. After a few minutes, Jayne began to calm down. "I can't believe you didn't hear any of that," she said. "She was right here with us!"

Jayne described to me how at first she could hear someone in the bathroom. "She was in there," Jayne said. "I could hear her, but then she came into the room with us! It was her, it was the midwife—I'm sure of it. I could hear her walking back and forth. She walked very quickly, kicking the inside of her floor-length dress as she went. Then suddenly she stopped and came over to the bed. I could feel her standing there looking down at me, but then the feeling began to fade away, and she was gone."

As the night went on I felt uneasy, and sleep would only come in broken segments. I began to worry about how I would make the long drive home if I didn't get enough sleep. Suddenly my eyes shot open as yet another sound broke the silence. This time it was something more human. It was the sound of a little boy and girl running down the hall, laughing as they passed our door. Next came the heavy footfalls of the man who followed them. He came only partway down the hall and stopped at our door. I half expected to hear him knock, but instead he turned and walked back the way he came and never returned.

I never thought to check the time, but I knew it was incredibly rude to let the children make so much noise at such a late hour. Perhaps my anger over the noise they made was distraction enough to prevent me from noticing how very strange this event really was, but nevertheless, I didn't notice.

In the morning when Jayne and I checked out, the young lady behind the counter politely asked if we slept well. "I haven't slept that good in a long time," Jayne responded.

"As for me, I rolled around all night long," I told her.

She smiled and said, "Men never sleep very good here. Did you have an experience?" I told her about the sound of someone banging on the pipes, and without a word she stepped out from behind the counter and walked over to a small television with a VCR and pushed a tape into it. The television came alive with the image of a woman from the cellar. She told a short story of how she could hear someone banging on the pipes only a few feet from her, yet no one was there to make the sound. I later learned that this is a common event at the Farnsworth House.

A few hours later, Jayne and I were on the road and well on our way home when she began digging through her bags and produced a small paperback book she had purchased from one of the souvenir shops. In it was another story of interest. The story she read was of a young artillery officer placed in charge of four cannons. The young officer was killed in the Battle of Gettysburg but some people claim to have heard his four cannons firing in the night. Could this have been the fireworks we heard?

Over all, the haunting I experienced at the Farnsworth House didn't seem as dramatic as I had hoped. However, after Jayne's incredible auditory experience, I felt it was worth another try. Perhaps next time the Sarah Black Room would prove more eventful.

One year later, Jayne and I did return to the Farnsworth House, and I was able to learn more about Jeremy and how very strange my experience really was!

CHAPTER THREE
GOOD MORNING, ANNA

Jayne and I kept our eyes peeled as we went, fearful we might miss 504 West Liberty Street, but the Spitzer House was easy to spot.

Painted a bright, two-toned peach, the former home of General Ceilan Milo Spitzer, which was built in 1890, stood out like a centerpiece among the other homes.

As we turned into the driveway, a sense of atmosphere washed over me. I felt as if an entire family had stepped outside to greet us, and although it was mid-February, I could easily imagine people in turn-of-the-century dress sitting out on the front porch in the warm evening air, sipping lemonade and enjoying each other's company.

Nothing about the house seemed very sinister at all, but I still had hope. As Jayne knocked on the large, black double doors, maybe they would open slowly, revealing the face of some demented servant who would beckon us in, saying, "We've been expecting you!"

Instead it was Janet Rogers who with her husband, Dale, purchased the house in 1990. She smiled brightly and welcomed us in as if we were old friends. I glanced around the room in hopes of finding some frightening hint of the paranormal, but instead my eyes focused in on none other than Santa himself, standing in the corner with his baseball equipment ready for a game.

I knew at that moment that haunted or not, this wasn't the sinister hell house I was hoping for, but rather a warm and friendly family home.

After getting settled into our room, Jayne and I took several pictures in various directions. We then stepped outside to get a few more of the front of the house. Now there would be little else to do but wait for the evening hours when our vigil would begin. Dinner and a movie helped to kill some time before returning at about ten o'clock. Jayne and I again settled into our room, this time for the night. It wasn't long before a new kind of energy filled the air. It was like that of a young girl excited to have a sleepover with her new friends. Or perhaps she was somehow aware that we had come to see her and was simply happy to have company of her own.

However, the feeling of energy may have been induced by the many dolls and teddy bears that decorated the room. This was, after all, Anna's Room, and it was filled with everything a young girl would like.

While sitting there among the many decorations, I didn't try to ignore the atmosphere that surrounded me, but I couldn't accept it as a physic experience either. I simply had to wait for something more substantial. We sat for a long time waiting for something to happen, but soon the atmosphere began to fade until the room seemed no different from any other. Before long, my hopes also began to fade, and boredom became our new companion. Watching the television in our room provided little entertainment, so Jayne and I sat talking late into the night.

Our conversation drifted from the paranormal to many other things, but all the while we kept alert for anything unusual. Soon, however, the lights would be turned off, and sleep would come easily even for me.

When the morning's first light came shining through the bedroom windows, calling me out of a deep sleep, the memory of last night's vigil wasn't far behind, and a wave of disappointment washed over me. The previous night had been uneventful, and I settled back into bed thinking about it. It was hard not to feel disappointed, but I knew that even in a location where paranormal activity has been well documented, nothing can ever be expected to happen, and the Spitzer House was no different.

I lay there staring at the ceiling for only a little bit longer before I remembered the coffee maker we found last night. I was eager to be on the road and headed for home, but a cup of coffee seemed like a good idea, and there wasn't any reason to wake Jayne just yet. Slipping out of bed, careful not to disturb her, I made my way to the coffee pot.

Glancing out of the bedroom windows, I could see the dusting of snow that had fallen during the night.

Below me a solitary car made its way down the empty street, leaving whirlwinds of snow in its wake. I wondered momentarily where he might be going so early on a Sunday morning, but looking down at the empty coffee pot in my hand I put it out of my mind. *The only thing I need right now is water,* I thought, but as I turned to look back at the bathroom, something else caught my attention. Grasping the coffee pot tightly, I stood there frozen with astonishment. The rocking chair next to the bed was quietly rocking back and forth, its movement steady as if it would never slow to a stop. "No way," I said out loud. Then laughing nervously, I walked the few short steps over to the chair, and reaching out, I stopped it. *This just can't be. I must have bumped into it when I got out of bed,* I thought. *But why don't I remember doing it?*

All at once I realized the mistake I had just made. What if I didn't bump the chair? I made it a rule to look for a logical explanation first, and only when no such explanation can be found will I consider the paranormal a possibility. But in this case I made what seemed logical the only possibility, and now without having timed the duration of the chair's movement or taking a photograph of it, I would never know how long it may have continued to rock or what a picture may have revealed.

It was unfortunate that such an opportunity may have been lost, but experience had also been gained, and I know now that a logical explanation may not be the correct answer to every question.

Soon Jayne began to stir. I had a cup of coffee ready for her, and we sat and talked for a while, but I never told her about the chair and how it seemed to move in a steady and deliberate motion. It may after all have been nothing more than my own clumsiness that caused the chair to rock back and forth, and so I never saw any reason to mention it. We talked a little while longer before I suggested we get going. "We still have a long drive ahead of us," I told her as I gathered up the empty coffee cups and threw them away.

Jayne stepped into the shower while I got dressed and packed up the few things we had brought with us. As I did, I could hear the sound of her voice from inside the bathroom. Something had startled her, but I couldn't tell what until she opened the door. She was smiling wide and excited. "The water just came on by itself! I got out of the shower and started getting dressed when the water in the sink just came on all by itself!"

Jayne was obviously expecting an equally excited response, but I could only look back at the rocking chair, which now sat motionless, and be reminded of how it seemed to move as though occupied and admit to myself that the logical explanation I once had now seemed more like an excuse for something I wasn't ready to accept. Jayne interrupted my thoughts, telling me again of how the water came on by itself, but I had no logical explanation to offer. "Things like that don't happen at home, do they?" I asked.

We gathered up our belongings and looked around the room one last time just to make sure we didn't forget anything. "Good-bye, Anna," I said. "I hope we can come to visit you again sometime."

Descending the stairs, we found Janet waiting patiently with breakfast ready. I really wanted nothing more than to be on my way, but Janet was a gracious host, and such an attitude seemed nothing more than rude and unkind.

In the end, I was glad we had chosen to stay; the breakfast was good, but the conversation was even better.

Janet was a very easy person to talk to and even more interesting to listen to. She told us about some of the things she had experienced while living in the house, and we talked until the morning hours were almost spent, but now it was time to get going. We thanked her for a pleasant evening, but before handing over our keys to our room, Jayne asked if it would be okay if she ran upstairs to use the bathroom before we left. "Of course," Janet replied, and with that Jayne was up the stairs and out of sight. Janet and I stood talking for only a short time before Jayne came walking back down.

Her expression was questioning. "Did you leave the door to our room open?" she asked.

"No, well I don't remember closing it, but I wasn't born in a barn," I said.

"Well, it was standing wide open when I got up there."

I heard Janet gasp. "Those doors close automatically," she whispered, as if speaking only to herself. The look on her face was one of genuine fright, and I knew if nothing else the stories she had told us must have been true.

The following day when our film had been developed, Jayne and I found something else of interest. Out of the five photographs we had taken in front of the house, three of them contained orbs, a small, misty white circle or ball of light believed by many to be spirit energy. In one photograph, seven orbs could be seen, three that seemed to drift near the front porch and four more in the driveway next to our car. Could this explain what I felt as we pulled into the driveway? We had also taken several pictures in our room, most of which were perfectly normal. However, in one photo, a misty white column of light could be seen standing behind the bathroom door.

Psychics and parapsychologists often refer to this as a vortex or portal used by spirits to move from this world to the next, and it could explain the poltergeist-like activity that occurred that morning.

In all, our visit to the Spitzer House wasn't particularly frightening or dramatic, but it was without a doubt interesting.

To anyone considering their first attempt at paranormal investigation, I recommend a stay at the Spitzer House. And stay for breakfast—you'll enjoy it.

CHAPTER FOUR

✦✦✦✦✦

RESPECT FOR THE DEAD

After a year-long wait, Jayne and I were finally able to return to the Farnsworth House. But this time we would be staying in the Sarah Black Room, said to be the most active room in the house. The gentleman who checked us in seemed delighted to inform us that our room had been unusually active the past few days. He then added that a psychic had recently been to the house, telling them, "Jeremy isn't alone. It seems he has a playmate, a little girl named Elisabeth." I remembered our last visit and the two children I heard running down the hall in the middle of the night. They ran laughing and playing with a burst of energy that at such a late hour seemed unusual even for children.

After Jayne and I had been shown to our room, I stepped back out into the hallway. Standing in front of the Catherine Sweeney Room, I looked in each direction and thought about the two children I heard run past our door to the end of the hall. Where had they gone? I wondered. I realized then that I should have heard them go into the Sarah Black Room, but they didn't.

They never ran upstairs or came back the way they had come. The laughter just suddenly stopped, and the hall became quiet. Seconds later, I heard the footsteps of a solitary man who walked only as far as our door where he stopped for a moment, turned, and walked away.

I smiled, thinking about that sleepless night one year ago. After having been told about Elisabeth, it made sense that I heard two children, but who was the solitary man, and what did he want? I could only shrug the question off and return to our room where Jayne had already begun taking pictures. As she turned in each direction, she spoke to her surroundings, trying to communicate with Jeremy. "Are you here with us?" she asked. "Would you like me to take your picture?" With every flash of her camera, she tried to make contact with him. I, however, had a different plan in mind. On our first visit, I noticed a picture hanging in the library; it was a photograph of our room that showed a misty white cloud drifting near the bed. I took the electromagnetic field meter I had brought with me out of my bag. An electromagnetic field meter, or EMF meter, is commonly used to detect energy fields in the atmosphere. Many people believe that spirit energy can also be detected by such a device, and so placing it on the canopy above the bed, I let the probe hang down. Now my trap was set! If an unseen presence came near the bed, an alarm built into the EMF meter would go off, giving me a chance to photograph it for myself.

By this time, Jayne had finished taking pictures around the room, and we agreed it was time for dinner, but before going out, I still had one thing left to do. I placed a voice-activated tape recorder on the bed near the EMF meter so that if anything should happen while we were away, the recorder would pick up the sound of the alarm, and I would know there had been some kind of activity in the room.

After dinner, Jayne and I stopped at a nearby souvenir shop. We wanted to get a map of the battlefield and go back to our room where we could select the different sites we wanted to investigate later that night. But the first thing I did when we got back to the room was check the tape recorder to see if anything had happened while we were away. The recorder hadn't picked up anything other than the faint sounds of traffic outside, and I began to feel impatient as a result. I looked around the room and spoke out loud to the surrounding atmosphere, just as Jayne had done earlier. But I didn't try to make contact with Jeremy. I spoke instead to the Confederate soldiers that are said to haunt the house. Taunting and teasing, I dared them to respond. "Come on, girls," I said, "let's see what you're made of."

"You better stop it," Jayne warned. "They can hear you!" The look of concern on her face was priceless, but the whole idea of teasing a ghost seemed too silly to continue, so instead I picked up the bag we brought back with us from the souvenir shop, and fishing around inside, I found the battlefield map we had purchased.

Jayne had decided to lay down for awhile and get some rest before going out to the battlefield. So I spread the map out on my side of the bed and began looking for areas with known paranormal activity. One site of particular interest was Spangler's spring, which is said to be haunted by a specter known as the lady in white. A young woman heartbroken over a failed romance took her own life there many years ago, and it's said that a phantom woman has been seen by many walking alone in the darkness. As my eyes continued to scan the map, I could feel the air around me getting heavy, but I was too involved in what I was looking at to pay attention. Instead I found another spot, a spot known as the wheat field. Union troops made their way across the small patch of land, completely unaware of the Confederate line hidden among the trees only a short distance away. Disaster struck with bloody results as the men became lost in a cloud of gun smoke and confusion. In the end, even the wheat that had been growing there was cut flat by Confederate rifle fire.

As I tried to imagine the terrible carnage and bloodshed that occurred in the wheat field that day, Jayne became restless and uneasy. Walking into the bathroom, she turned the light on. "It seems to be getting a little bit creepy in there," she told me. But I was still too caught up in the map to notice. I had found yet another place, a small stream nicknamed Plum Run. Once filled with clear water, it soon ran red with the blood of Confederate soldiers as their repeated attacks on Little Round Top continued to fail. Only yards away from that stream stands a cluster of boulders needed by the Confederates to continue the relentless assault. The vantage point was finally taken by the Confederate Army only after what must have been some of the most fierce and chaotic fighting that occurred during the Battle of Gettysburg, earning it the nicknamed Devil's Den.

"Can't you feel that?" Jayne interrupted.

"What do you mean?" I asked looking up at her.

"The bathroom, it's really starting to get creepy in there!"

"Yeah, I see what you mean," I said, looking toward the bathroom, but again I focused my mind on the map in front of me, unable to clearly understand what was happening.

As I looked down, my attention settled on the mile-long path now known as Pickett's Charge. I was completely absorbed in the map as I tried to imagine that final day of the battle. Three divisions, a total of twelve thousand men, would attack the Union center, breaking their line of defense and ultimately bringing about the defeat of the Army of the Potomac. But as the men stood awaiting their orders, not one among them didn't understand the advantage their enemy had over them, or the courage with which they would defend themselves. On that day, Union lead would rain down on them, and for many, it would be their last.

In my mind, I could hear the murmured prayers and see the men glancing back and forth, looking into the eyes of their brothers, friends, and neighbors, hoping to find courage and strength as the commanding officer gave his only words of advice. "Make haste across that field, boys, as I am certain today you're going to catch hell!" And then the order came. General Armistead raised his sword high in the air and spoke in a voice all could hear. "For your lands, for your homes, for your sweethearts, for Virginia, forward march!" From the very first, Union cannons took aim, watching their every step, and soon the thunder of artillery began. Cannonballs screamed across the sky, hammering them relentlessly as they began the mile-long march. Soon they would reach Emmetsburg Road where the futility of their charge became obvious. Like marching through a swarm of lethal hornets, bullets flew at them from every direction, and men fell on all sides. Short-range cannons filled with mini balls, nuts, bolts, and anything else that would kill exploded. But now in their few they made it to the Union center where rifles fired at pointblank range and the fighting became hand to hand. Despite the courageous charge of twelve thousand Confederate soldiers, the Union line would not break. The sons of Virginia were turned back; Pickett's Charge had failed.

Now the crippled and tattered remains of the Confederate army turned from the battlefield, leaving those who had fallen behind. One newspaper reporter of the day described the scene by saying, "In the wake of the Confederate retreat, the dead and dying littered the ground as do the withered leaves of autumn."

"Keith, Keith!" I could hear my wife's voice reaching out to me from some other world.

"What?" I asked, looking up from the map.

"Look at the bathroom!"

"What about it?"

"Don't you remember? I turned the light on because it was getting creepy in there, but it's off now!" Looking into the bathroom, which was now just as dark as she said it would be, I could feel the energy she had been complaining about. A strong sense of presence seemed to grow and swirl within the darkened room, and the feeling that someone was watching us was undeniable.

But it was still necessary to check the light. I needed to know if the bulb had simply burned out or if it was turned off at the switch. A pair of eyes seemed to glare at me from somewhere within the darkness as I entered the bathroom. Searching for the light switch, it came as no surprise when I found it in the off position. The sensation Jayne had been complaining about was now overwhelming, and it was impossible for me to stay in the bathroom for even a moment longer. Forced from the darkened room, I went back to the bed where I had been looking at the map, but now I was unable to focus my attention on anything other than the bathroom.

What Jayne had once described as a creepy feeling had grown into something menacing as it began to spill into our room and make its way toward us. "Oh shit!" Jayne shouted as the alarm built into my EMF meter began to scream. Whatever it was that had been watching us from the bathroom was now standing directly in front of us! Helplessly I looked up at the EMF meter above me. It was as if I had been caught in my own trap, and something unimaginable was about to happen, but instead the alarm suddenly stopped, and the feeling of presence began to fade. Our nightmare ended as quickly as it began. Laughing, I looked over at Jayne. "What the hell was that?"

"That's what happens when you talk shit to a ghost," she answered.

After the feeling of presence that filled our room faded completely away, the room seemed somehow empty and drained of its energy. Like a sudden storm that had come and gone, I knew it wouldn't be back again, and for the rest of the night, our room was no different from any other.

During the long drive home, I had plenty of time to think about the visitor who came to our room and the feeling of malice that came along with it. But I also had time to think about the Battle of Gettysburg and the men who fought there. By the thousands they died for what they believed in, but in the end they were driven back in defeat. I also took some time to remember the grief-stricken father who is said to pace up and down the hallway just outside our door. And the midwife whose soul still lingers in the air, held to earth by her sense of responsibility for the mothers of Gettysburg.

At the end of life when the body falls away and the soul is left to flutter in the open air, what more could remain but our thoughts, hopes, dreams, and every emotion that once made our hearts beat faster? Perhaps our visitor wasn't angry over the things I had said, but that I didn't understand what happened those three days of July 1863, and that he was a man whose life once held meaning.

CHAPTER FIVE

∙◆◆◆∙

THE ONES THEY LEFT BEHIND

Mansfield Reformatory would be our first official ghost hunt, and Jayne and I were eager to get there. But as we left the Cleveland area and the landscape became more and more rural, I began to wonder what it would be like for a convicted felon, filled with despair as he takes that long bus ride to the reformatory, a place where he will trade the rolling hills and blue skies I was looking at for a small, dark prison cell. Perhaps a younger man never having been in this kind of trouble before, might look to his fellow passengers, but their eyes would be cold and empty, void of any sympathy or compassion. Turning his head back to the window, he would watch the scenery pass by and wish to God he could turn back the hands of time.

When Jayne and I came to the end of Reformatory Road and the prison stood up from behind the tall chain-link fence and revealed itself, I thought again about my imaginary convict and how the prison might look to him. Not as a place of judgment, for that decision has already been made, but a symbol of unyielding power and control. A place where he will learn to obey the iron will of prison guards and evade the jealous brutality of his fellow inmates.

I realized then that I would not only be investigating the paranormal world of dark shadows, spirits, and the ghosts that linger behind the stone walls of this abandoned prison, but the prison itself and the lives that were spent there, held in the grasp of iron bars.

After parking the car and stretching the stiffness out of my legs, Jayne and I went inside to join the group of people that had already begun to accumulate. Scanning the room, I could see the look of anticipation and excitement on the faces of the people who had come to explore the prison. In one corner of the room, a small group of people stood talking among themselves, and a young girl with them giggled nervously as she began to fidget with her camera. In every direction, I saw people adjusting and checking their equipment as they shuffled their feet back and forth, restlessly waiting for the night to begin. Nearby, a nurse described to her companions one of the many experiences she had while working the nightshift at the hospital, and I thought back to the night my son was born. Jayne lay as comfortable as possible in her bed, and I sat on the couch across the room from her.

We had only just settled into the room and finished speaking to each other when I clearly heard a young boy's voice at the foot of her bed. Sounding cheerful and happy, I heard the words, "Hi, baby!" Then the voice seemed to turn directly to me and say, "Hi, Papa!" Quickly I glanced around the room, searching for the person who had just spoken to me, but found no one.

"You heard that too, didn't you?" Jayne asked. We both agreed the voice was that of a young boy, yet we were alone in the room!

As I looked back at the nurse and her companions, I was glad to see that I would be in the company of people who would take the event seriously and not treat the whole affair like some childish game of trick or treat. In fact, it seemed I was surrounded by people who shared my interest in the paranormal, and as I stood there, my sense of anticipation began to grow. Just then I felt my wife tapping my shoulder. I took the nametag she held out to me and signed the guest list. Now there was nothing more to do than get in line for the guided tour.

The tour took us throughout the prison, but with daylight still shining through the barred windows, our experience was less than haunting. It was, however, interesting to see the inside of a prison and the remnants left behind after its evacuation. Walking along the rows of cells, we eventually came to one where the inmate who once occupied it had scratched the word "welcome" into the cement just outside the door. The joke really wasn't very funny or imaginative, but the mental picture I had of him laying on the floor of his cell, hour after hour carving each letter into the cement, gave real meaning to the phrase "doing time." Moving along, we finally found ourselves in the section of the prison where the warden lived. It seemed incomprehensible to me that anyone would choose to live within the confines of a prison. The entire area was cold and barren, without even a trace of human warmth. We did, however, find one room of special interest; it was the bedroom where the warden's wife was killed.

She had been rummaging through the closet when a shoe box containing a loaded revolver fell from the top shelf. As it struck the floor, the gun inside discharged, killing her instantly. But the accident may have been too sudden, and her death too unexpected for her to clearly perceive it as a reality. As her body lay lifeless on the floor beneath her feet, she simply continued with her daily routine, unaware that her life had been cut short. Now after so many years have passed, the room contains nothing more than peeling paint and debris, but on occasion, the fragrant aroma of a woman's perfume can be detected in the air, and the chilling sound of her voice softly singing still echoes about the room.

After leaving the bedroom, our tour continued until we came to the end of a long hallway where someone had carved his name into the woodwork above us. It read *Brooks was here*, and just below that, *so was Red*.

Our tour guide explained to us that the movie *Shawshank Redemption* had been filmed here, and this was the room where Brooks, unable to cope with life on the outside, committed suicide. Morgan Freeman, who had played the part of Red, also carved his name into the woodwork just before setting out to find his friend Andy.

It was fascinating to be in the very spot where Hollywood filmed the movie and also to stand in the footsteps of some of its more well-known actors, but now it was time to begin the hunt, and people were starting to split up into private groups. As they moved off in their chosen directions, the lights began to go out. Section by section, they went off until Jayne and I found ourselves alone in the dark. The beams of our flashlights sliced through the blackness as we slowly made our way back to the cell block we had just come from. But now in the darkness, it almost seemed possible to hear the sounds of the men in lock up. They whispered, coughed, and rustled about, watching us make our way from cell to cell. As we walked along, we began taking pictures in every direction, hopeful we might catch something on film that we were otherwise unable to see. The random flash of our cameras momentarily illuminated our way like lightning across a midnight sky until finally we found ourselves in solitary confinement, where in the past, two murders and a suicide had taken place.

One prisoner no longer able to accept the terms of his incarceration took his own life. Right in the very spot where Jayne and I stood, a prison guard taken by surprise was brutally murdered by an inmate. On another occasion, prison officials decided to increase the punishment factor of solitary confinement by forcing two inmates into each cell. But the pressure of being forced to share a cell that had been originally designed for only one man at a time proved too much for at least one inmate, and in the morning when guards opened the door of his cell, they found he had strangled his cellmate to death and stuffed the body under his bunk.

The entire area is said to be rife with paranormal activity, and this would soon prove to be a valid claim. As we walked along, we became aware of other people in the area. Around the corner on the other side of solitary where the suicide had taken place, five people stood arguing over the existence of an orb-like light they had seen. One man among them who claimed to have seen it described it as being red in color. "It was following us," he said, "but when I noticed it, it stopped momentarily and then began moving away from us until it vanished from view."

"Are you sure it wasn't just a reflection?" another man who was with them asked. "The light on my camcorder is red. Maybe that's what you saw."

But a woman interrupted the conversation, saying, "No, I saw it too! It was three dimensional. It didn't shine on the floor or any of the walls. It just hung there in midair for a moment and then darted away like it didn't want to be seen." The five people we encountered stood there looking back and forth at one another, mystified by what they had seen as they talked among themselves.

Jayne and I slipped quietly past and continued on our way, secretly hoping the red orb would reveal itself to us. Although it never made another appearance, on our second visit to the penitentiary, I had my own experience in solitary confinement. We decided not to join the tour group, after having been there once before; we felt we knew our way around well enough to go alone. First we made our way to the warden's quarters and found the haunted bedroom. It was dark and quiet, and though a sense of presence seemed to drift about the room, there was no trace of a woman's perfume in the air or the sound of her voice softly singing.

And so, undeterred, we continued on our way exploring every hallway that captured our imagination until we had finally made our way down to solitary confinement, where the tour guide was talking to the people in his group. He pointed out the third cell, telling them of the murder that had taken place there. I stood by patiently waiting for them to move along so we could get past and continue with our own investigation. But as I listened to the tour guide's description of the murder, my attention was drawn to the fourth cell where a feeling of rage seemed to scream out to me, "I'm in here!" The hostility and malevolence I experienced was intense, but above all, it was focused—and focused on me!

I watched the group of people walk past, and not a single one of them so much as glanced into the empty cell.

Even Jayne, who began to follow them, was oblivious to the energy I had become aware of, and I realized immediately why. The entity that occupied cell four was trying to make contact with me and me alone!

As I walked past the cell, I was reminded of a time when I was a small boy. A vicious dog belonging to one of our neighbors stood on hind legs, his chain pulled tight, and his teeth bared as he growled and barked at me in a furious rage.

Now in the darkness of solitary confinement, I was filled with the same feeling of dread, and although the cell door stood wide open, I knew that in his world he could not pass through it. He was somehow detained like the dog that made its appearance in so many of my childhood nightmares. As his rage reached out for me from behind the iron bars, I turned to simply hurry past. I then took a few steps back until I was directly in front of the empty cell and aimed my camera. "Say cheese," I said as I took the picture. When the film was developed. one faint orb appeared floating about a foot above the bunk. Was it him? Or simply a tiny speck of dust on the camera lens, collaborating with my own imagination to make the whole incident seem real?

Most skeptics will say that all orbs are nothing more than dust, and the imagination is a powerful thing. But the energy I felt beaming out at me from the fourth cell was intense. It screamed at me as if I were its only chance for freedom, or perhaps revenge for the forgotten years of incarceration.

Later that night, however, when Jayne and I returned to solitary confinement, the menacing sense of rage I felt before had begun to fade and now did little more than glower at me as it dwindled away.

Toward the end of the night, Jayne and I encountered yet another person who claimed to have had an experience in the area of solitary confinement. A young girl held her hand up to her face as she told us of something unseen that caressed her cheek. Perhaps her experience was the result of a spider's web and a bit of wishful thinking, or maybe the murdered guard who still makes his rounds held out his hand in a lonely attempt at making her acquaintance. Nevertheless, Mansfield Reformatory is filled with dark secrets and rumors of torture, murder, and suicide. It is a place where every darkened hallway leads to another adventure.

We explored the abandoned prison and its many points of interest, from the tormented souls and ghosts that looked down upon us from the cells above, to the glimmer of Hollywood. Whether you've come in search of the paranormal or just something out of the ordinary, Mansfield Reformatory will spark the interest and imagination of just about anyone.

In the morning when the sky began to turn from black to a light shade of blue, I yawned deeply and opened the can of energy drink I had saved for the drive home. As we pulled out of the parking lot, I looked up at my rearview mirror and watched the reformatory shrink and fall away. As I did, I thought one last time of my imaginary convict and what his fate may have been. Maybe he did his time and found his way home again, or perhaps like the prisoner in cell four he was left behind, forgotten, sentenced to forever.

CHAPTER SIX

DID YOU HEAR THE SCREAMING?

When the Genesee County home opened its doors in 1827, it began a long but infamous history.

Built with all good intentions, it was the last resort of the elderly, orphans, homeless people, and also the insane. Standing much as it has for nearly two hundred years, it was for some anything but a safe or comfortable haven.

Children who were in good health could expect that for a price they would be handed over to local farmers and business men to serve as laborers. Those who lay dying from tuberculosis were often abused and tormented by the head nurse, a woman who was said to be a practitioner of the black arts, and soon rumors to that effect began to circulate. Stories of black witchcraft, devil worship, and infant sacrifice were whispered throughout the community, and such stories lasted well into the 1900s.

Although stories told about the old county home continued to spread and live on, many of its occupants did not. Whether from advanced age, tuberculosis, or some other incurable disease, many of the people who came to reside there never left. Historical records show that over a thousand people died on the property, and their unmarked and forgotten graves freckle the surrounding land.

Locals drive cautiously past as they ponder the stories that have been told around the county for years—stories of a haunted lunatic asylum where spirits roam the grounds, bemoaning their forgotten lives. Mysterious lights move through the vacant building, and an apparition is said to peer down from the windows above, though everyone knows the old county home has stood empty for nearly twenty years.

The property has since been purchased and in 2004 was renamed Rolling Hills Country Mall. Now like a modern-day oasis, the first floor offers its own café and rooms filled with beautiful handcrafted furniture. But venturing through the rest of the building is like walking into a world where memories live on, memories that some say are better left forgotten.

Paranormal investigators report disembodied voices, knockings, chairs moving about, and doors that open and then close again by themselves. You may experience a tap on the shoulder as someone unseen whispers your name. And on one occasion, a full-body apparition was caught on film.

"I can't wait to get there," I said. "I mean who wouldn't want to go to a place like that and spend the night alone in the dark?"

Jayne smiled back at me and shook her head. "Keep your eyes on the road," she warned. The next few miles went by in silence, but then Jayne leaned forward in her seat. "I'm pretty sure it's around here somewhere," she said. Then only a moment later, she pointed across the dashboard to the left side of the road. "There it is; that's Rolling Hills."

But the building I saw looked a little out of place in its rural setting and somehow reminded me of an old man boasting of his glory days when he was considered large and official. The old county home was smaller than I expected, but this could stand as testimony to its age. When the home was built in 1827, the area would have been less densely populated, and there would have been no need for a larger building. Feeling a little disappointed by its size, I pulled the car into the gravel parking lot and drove all the way to its end where I found a secluded spot. After shutting off the engine, I looked back at the old county home and reconsidered its size. A more massive structure would make it easy for us to separate ourselves from the other investigators, but its paranormal activity would be more scattered, lessoning our chances of being in the right place at the right time. I got out of the car with all of this on my mind and walked around back to open the hatch. While Jayne gathered equipment out of the car, I glanced off to my right at the surrounding landscape and the rolling hills the country mall was named for. But I was distracted by what I saw only a few yards away.

There, rising up from its otherwise flat surroundings, was a mound. It was completely covered by grass as though it had been there a good many years, and suspiciously, it fit the dimensions of a grave. I looked back again at the building we were about to investigate and after a little more consideration decided that Rolling Hills and its infamous history offered mounting possibilities.

It didn't take long before we had signed the guest list and were on the guided tour. Walking down the darkened corridor, we made our first stop at a room that had a surprising history. It was a jail cell. Our tour guide explained to us that there was a time when the room was used as a holding cell for female prisoners on their way to the New York State Penitentiary. The room looked no different from any of the other rooms, but upon further examination, it was possible to see where iron bars once covered the windows, iron bars that had only recently been removed and could still be found leaning against the wall.

He also told us that, though he himself never experienced anything of a paranormal nature connected to that particular room, other people claim to have heard the sound of a mad woman screaming in the night. Looking into the room, I wondered why only women were brought there. But the thought was interrupted when my imagination introduced me to the image of a women clad in blue denim, her wrists adorned by dangling chains, her eyes dark and sunken inward from the years of madness. She bared her teeth in a grimacing smile, cursing and threatening me as she declared her innocence and demanded to be released. *What a bonus*, I thought, but looking into the eyes of the people around me, it was obvious they also had envisioned the same screaming, banshee-like phantom and were somewhat troubled by the idea.

Our next stop was a completely different matter. This room did bother me, and it bothered me a lot. Our next stop was the tuberculosis ward, a room where the atmosphere was dark and heavy, to say the very least.

Tuberculosis was a disease that in its time was considered the modern-day plague, and there was only one expected outcome. The orphaned children who suffered from this dreadful affliction lay amid strange surroundings without so much as a mother's hand to hold. In the darkness, they lay quiet and still, fearful that any noise they made would attract the attention of the head nurse, a woman who would punish and torment them till their remaining days ran out and there was nothing left but another unmarked grave.

The owners of Rolling Hills have tried to ease the suffering of any child spirits who might remain in the room, still fearful and hiding, by decorating it in the fashion of good Saint Nick. A Christmas tree stands in one corner of the room while Santa's workshop fills another. There is even a sleigh complete with reindeer and many other things that bring cheer to the hearts of children.

But the decorations are a thin disguise for the fear and cruelty that once existed there.

Our tour guide went on with his description of the room and its history, but as he did, he warned us that photographs taken in this room may reveal startling results. Unfortunately, these results can be easily explained. Over the years, warm, humid air has caused the wood paneling to warp, and the camera's flash will reflect at odd angles, making it appear as though some smoky apparition has been caught on film. However, rumor has it that one photograph taken in the room revealed something that wasn't so easy to explain. Standing in front of Santa's sleigh was the faint outline of a small boy dressed in clothes that date back to the early 1900s.

After leaving the tuberculosis ward, the tour made its way throughout the building. We visited places such as the kitchen with its freezers where meat was delivered and stored. We also paid a visit to the electroshock therapy room where patients were taken for treatment. But the grand finale lay waiting for us in the attic rooms above. These rooms were used as sleeping quarters for the nurses who were on staff at the old county home, and it was widely believed they were all members of a satanic cult, a cult that may have performed its rituals right there in the area we were about to explore. The lack of windows made it much darker than any of the floors below us, and the ceiling sloped downward, taking on the contour of the roof, which provided a feeling of claustrophobia.

We walked along the narrow hallways, passing the oddly shaped corners and storage areas that seemed filled with dreadful secrets and the knowledge of things once kept there. Each room we came to felt as though it maintained a personality of its own, but without the benefit of psychic ability, I can only describe it as distinctly feminine, yet hard and unforgiving.

Our tour continued until eventually we made our way to the other side of the building where we entered the administrator's room.

Situated near the door was an old piano, said to be the center of paranormal activity in the room. Our tour guide told us that the administrator's favorite pastime was playing it, until one night a fatal heart attack took his life, and he died in that very room, possibly sitting at the piano.

While experimenting with EVP or electronic voice phenomena, many paranormal investigators have reported harsh language ordering them away from the instrument. Others have reported a tug on their hair or clothing and an icy-cold breath of air drifting about the room. I wish I could say I had a similar experience in what is now referred to as the piano room, but the room and piano both seemed flat and lifeless. Also, none of the photographs we had taken there revealed anything out of the ordinary. But the rooms we visited previously did emit a strong sense of atmosphere, and a photo taken in one of the nurse's rooms showed an oddly shaped light anomaly.

After leaving the attic, our tour group split up into its own personal fragments, and Jayne and I found ourselves once again alone in the darkness.

We wandered about the old building until we had somehow managed to find ourselves on a floor that was completely vacant. With no one else in sight, Jayne hurried along, convinced she could feel a presence somewhere down the hall. I followed along, but at a slower more leisurely pace. I lagged further and further behind until I came to a room that called out to me in a sad and lonely voice.

The room was small but could probably hold three beds if one were placed on the opposing side of the room facing the windows, and this was the area that drew my attention. I could easily imagine a young boy who would have been no more than seven years old, bedridden due to illness or perhaps punishment. My heart grew heavy as I thought of my own son and how this boy must have felt, laying there day after day staring out the window, wishing he could be free of his prison-like surroundings.

Looking toward the windows, my mind's eye was filled with a vision, a vision I'm certain belonged to someone else. The windows once blackened by the night were now alight with blue sky and cotton-ball clouds, and I could feel his sense of freedom and elation as he ran across the fields just outside. I wasn't sure, however, if he had finally been permitted to go outside and play, or was he running away from this awful place? But as I looked back to the small, dark room I was standing in, I began to feel more and more that this was something that had never actually happened, that it was only a little boy's wish, a wish that never came true.

I stepped back out into the hall where I found Jayne and called her back to the room. "Can you feel it?" I asked. "I think there's someone in here."

Jayne shook her head in an uncertain manner. "Yeah, I guess so," she replied, and we began taking pictures in every direction. When developed, none of them revealed anything, but our attempts at an EVP did! After we finished taking photographs around the room, I brought out a tape recorder, and we began asking questions of the atmosphere around us. Jayne first asked, "Is there anyone here?" But no response came. She then asked, "Can you hear me?" Again, no response. "Is there anyone here who would like to talk to us?" Still, no response. "We would really like to talk to you. Would you like to talk to us?"

Then a response came. It was the voice of a small boy. "Yeah," was all it said.

Jayne continued asking questions. "Are you a boy or a girl?" But there was no response. "How old are you? Did you die here?" But again she got no response.

Then I stepped in with a question that seemed obvious to me. "How long have you been in this room?"

An answer came instantly, but now the voice sounded angry and frustrated. "I don't know!"

Jayne continued asking questions, but no further response ever came, and soon we left the room with its lonely captive still inside.

We wandered the darkened halls of the old county home for a long time before we came to a room that was surrounded by windows. To me it seemed totally inactive, but we began taking pictures anyway. Then Jayne froze with her hand in the air, signaling me to wait. "Did you hear that?" she asked. "It sounded like someone moving furniture!" Following her out the door, she led me a short distance down the hall to an empty room. "It came from in here," she said. But the room was quiet now and contained no furniture or people to have moved it.

Though the entire area still seemed inactive to me, Jayne insisted the room down the hall was active. And so when we returned to it, I suggested we use the tape recorder again, but she was eager to use the divining rods she had brought with her.

Divining rods are a simple tool often used to locate and communicate with spirits. Consisting of two copper wire rods, each one mounted on a swivel, they're held out in front of the user; the rods then cross or widen to indicate a positive or negative response. With her divining rods held out in front of her, Jayne asked her first question. "Is there anyone here who would like to communicate with us?"

Her rods immediately crossed, giving a yes answer. She then let her left arm fall to her side and lifted her right hand high up over her head. "Where are you?" she asked, and the rod she held up began to spin in a clockwise rotation, indicating we were surrounded by spirit energy! She then asked, "Where is the spirit I'm talking to now?" I watched in amazement as the rod suddenly stopped, pointing to one corner of the room. Jayne again held both rods out in front of her and asked, "Are you a woman?"

As the rods widened, she looked back at me. "It's a man," she said. "Are you a young man?" The rods widened again. "Are you very old?" This time the rods crossed, giving a yes response. "Did you die here?" Again the rods crossed. "Will you tell us your name?" Yes! The spirit's final response provided us with an exciting opportunity. In the recent past, the state of New York donated a complete and documented list of names identifying all those who had died at the old county home, making it easy for us to check any name the spirit might give us against historical records.

Jayne's method for learning the spirit's name was a simple one. She would recite the alphabet, and her rods should cross on the first letter of his name. She would then recite the alphabet a second time to receive the second letter and then a third time for the third letter, and so on and so on until the spirit had spelled out his full name. I never considered Ouija boards, Tarot cards, or divining rods to be much more than unscientific hocus pocus, so when they failed to produce anything more than gibberish, I laughed and said, "It figures we would get a spook who can't spell."

"Don't make fun," Jayne snapped back at me. "He might have lived a long time ago when illiteracy was a lot more common." Again she held the rods out in front of her, this time asking, "Would you like to try again?"

But the rods widened abruptly, spinning completely around, as if to shout, "No!"

Afterward, the rods would render no response to any question asked. "He's gone now," Jayne said. "I think we offended him."

Soon voices and footsteps could be heard coming down the hall, and two men suddenly appeared standing in the doorway. "You guys see any ghosts around here?" I asked in a joking manner.

"No," the older of the two men said with a broad smile, "but earlier a bunch of us heard furniture being moved around."

"Where at?"

"Right down the hall," he said, pointing toward the same room Jayne had taken me to only a few minutes before.

Jayne and I wished the two men luck as we headed out the door, our sights set on the café downstairs. We had spent most of the night wandering through the old building, and it was time to sit down with a cup of coffee.

When we entered the little café, I was surprised to find it so crowded, mostly by people who were too excited by the things they had experienced to sit down and relax. They stood around in a small crowd, turning the café into a gathering place where people could come and talk about their experiences and show off the digital photos they had taken. While we were there, we met a nurse who was a bit upset by a small group of people who were somewhat loud and obnoxious. "Some people don't understand the significance of what we're doing here," I said. "They just think it's a game of trick or treat, but fortunately for us, they usually don't stay very long." She nodded in agreement, but I could tell she was still a little annoyed by their selfish nature. It wasn't hard to change the atmosphere of the conversation though; I simply asked her if she had any luck.

"A little," she said. "I got a few orbs in the tuberculosis ward and then a few more upstairs in the attic."

"We had some luck too," I said, telling her about the voice we got on tape.

She told us she was familiar with the room we were in, and the last time she came to Rolling Hills, she had a similar EVP experience. "I was able to pick up the name Michael," she said.

After finishing our coffee, we wished our new friend luck and excused ourselves. This time we made our way to the tuberculosis ward, or as it is sometimes referred to, the Christmas room. We found a couple of chairs near the sleigh and decided it might be a good idea to spend the rest of the night sitting down, waiting for someone or something to come to us. I took a base reading with an EMF meter and then scanned the room with night vision, but the energy level in the room was low, and I felt certain there would be no further activity tonight. I sat patiently, but before long my mind began to wander. I thought about the child spirits who are said to haunt the room and wondered if they were aware of my presence, and could they really see the decorations that surrounded them? Or perhaps to them the room was still a grim place, filled with the sick and dying. Using night vision, I scanned the room one more time, but to no avail; the room was empty and lifeless as if the children who haunt it had been drawn back to the world they came from. I took a deep breath and released it as a sigh, and then suddenly a loud shriek rippled through the night air. Jayne's body became rigid, and her eyes were wide. "What the hell was that?" she asked. But the sound I heard was too sudden and had escaped my ability to reason. The sound was like something I had never heard before, and without warning, it came again. Jayne's eyes were still wide with fright as she leaned forward in her chair. "That sounded like a scream!" she said.

I was still unable to identify the sound, but my wife's excitement was both thrilling and compelling. Suddenly the scream came again. The loud shrieking sound we heard filled the air around us, and I had only one thought. *It's the woman in blue denim!*

Jayne was frozen in her seat as I jumped up and headed toward the door. I ran out into the hall, looking for anyone else who might have heard it, and was immediately approached by a man and two women. "Did you hear someone scream?" the first of the two women asked.

But before I could answer, the second woman had already begun asking where the sound had come from. "I don't know," I said. "My wife and I were in the Christmas room when we heard it, but the sound seemed to come from everywhere."

Just then a third woman appeared, standing in the doorway of a room once used to store meat. She had a puzzled look on her face as she stood there. "I didn't hear anything," she said.

"You didn't hear any of that?" I asked.

"It was a woman screaming," the others told her, and the man with them also claimed he could feel the presence of a woman just before it all began.

But she shook her head. "I don't think it was a scream," she said sheepishly. We all stared blankly as she walked over to the first of two freezers positioned in the room. "Did it sound like this?" she asked. As she pulled the door open, the rubber seal at the bottom scraped across the tiled floor, creating a loud chirping sound, but everyone agreed it wasn't what they heard. "How about this?" she asked, opening the second freezer door. This time, the sound we heard was a loud shriek that seemed to fill the air around us, and the sound that followed it was one of disappointment.

The mystery was solved; there was no screaming woman. But we went home knowing the truth; that's what really matters. I do believe, however, that spirits and memories from long ago still roam the halls of the old county home, and if you're looking for a paranormal experience of your own, I recommend a visit to Rolling Hills Country Mall.

CHAPTER SEVEN

AMONG THE DIRE SHADOWS

After crossing the Ohio River, Jayne and I had no trouble finding the town of Moundsville, but surprisingly enough, we had even less trouble finding the prison. I expected a long drive down some wooded country road, but one right turn and a few streets later, we found it, the West Virginia State Penitentiary!

My first thought was what the cost of living might be. After all, not many people would be comfortable living across the street from a prison, especially one with such a violent history. Yet there it was right smack dab in the middle of town like some notorious shopping mall for crime and violence.

My next thought concerning location was Alcatraz and how it had been described to me. Alcatraz is situated on a small island just across the bay from San Francisco, and they say that on a calm night, gentle breezes would sometimes carry the smell of home cooking and the sounds of traffic across the water to the inmates, who could only peer through tiny slit-like windows at the sparkling jewel box of lights.

Surely the inmates of Alcatraz were tormented by the vision of freedom that could be seen just across the bay. But here in West Virginia, freedom was no further away than the other side of a stone wall, and I'm certain they could hear the sounds of traffic, perhaps even the distant ring of a school bell and the voices of children as they made their way home.

Looking up at the blue sky above me, I began to feel their loss of freedom, and a deep sadness washed over me. It was a terrible place, and I could feel it in the air around me.

The West Virginia State Penitentiary was built in 1866, and by the time it closed its doors in 1995, it had earned its place as one of the most violent and bloody prisons in the history of the United States. Over the 129 years of its operation, the prison saw as many as one thousand deaths, but only one hundred of these were sanctioned executions; the other nine hundred were the result of murder and suicide.

My wife and I joined the line of people waiting to sign in, and soon after that, the guided tour began. Every area we visited—every hallway, room, and corridor—seemed to bare its own tale of violence and bloodshed. Even the dining hall became the scene of one of the prison's most violent outbursts when in 1986 sixteen prison guards were taken hostage in a riot that lasted seventy-two hours.

Prison officials and fellow guards could do little as the sounds of tortured screams echoed down the long, dark halls. But at last, after three days, the violence had ended, and the sixteen guards were released unharmed. The mystery of who it was that had been screaming was soon cleared up as details of the riot became known. Demands made by inmates were for better food and longer visitation, but the real reason for the uprising was much darker.

The riot that occurred in 1986 was only a distraction, a distraction that gave access to three fellow inmates who had been accused of squealing. They were the worst of rats, giving information to guards concerning everything from contraband to escape plans. But now they lay in a pool of blood, silenced forever.

Maintenance is another reputedly haunted area, and I was about to have my first experience of the night. Our tour guide took us outside and then to a door at the rear of the prison where we found steps leading downward. The rooms were dark and getting darker by the minute, but we were eager to hear what the tour guide had to say, so we crowded in as quickly as we could.

"This is maintenance," she said, "and sadly, it seemed, the eternal home of R. D. Wallings. R.

D. was a man of privilege. He had no cell but instead lived in the maintenance area without bars or locks and was free to walk the yard at will. He also had the best food and many other favors extended to him by prison officials. These privileges, however, didn't come without being earned. R. D. didn't just work as the prison maintenance man; he also served as the sewer rat! If toilets began backing up, it could create an emergency situation, and R. D. didn't hesitate to jump in and do whatever it took to get the system flowing again. R. D. worked for the privileges he had, but compared to others, he lived the good life, and soon ignorance and jealously would bring it to an end.

"Six other inmates who felt his life was a little better than it should be entered the maintenance area armed with sheet steel knives. What happened next could be described using words like filleted, decapitated, and eviscerated. For weeks after the murder, guards positioned in the watchtower nearby would sound the alarm and say they had seen someone walking in the yard near the maintenance area, but no one was ever found. Before long, they simply accepted it as the ghost of R. D."

Our tour moved around to the other side of a fence in the area where the death house once stood. But as the tour guide spoke, my mind began to wander, and as it did, I saw something from the corner of my eye. It was a man with long, straight hair walking toward the door we first came out of. His form was gray and faceless, and he walked at a hurried pace as though responding to some urgency, but I never saw him reach the door. Instead he simply vanished among the surrounding shadows cast by the now setting sun.

I had little time to wonder who he was before I became distracted by the movement of people around me. As they began walking away, I felt obligated to follow, but I didn't forget about the man I had seen. He was still fresh in my mind when our tour guide told us of a roving phantom known as the shadow man.

"Many visitors to the prison claim to have seen the dark figure of a man," she said, "and they always describe him in much the same way. He's tall and slender but dark and colorless like the shadows he's said to emerge from. Sometimes he's found standing, watching you, while other times he's seen walking away. But in every case, when noticed, he seems to fade away or simply vanish!"

I looked over at my wife and whispered in her ear, "I think I saw him!"

Jayne turned and looked at me her eyes wide. "You saw him?"

"Yeah," I said, "when we were outside, I watched him walk across the yard right behind us, and then he was just gone!"

The group of people we were with began moving again. We followed them to a place called administrative segregation.

Administrative segregation was also referred to as the Alamo because it was considered the last stand for inmates who were too dangerous to share a cell or mingle with the general population, and guards knew to keep their distance and never turn their backs. If given a chance, prisoners locked up in the Alamo would attack them in any way they could, lashing out at them with homemade weapons or by mixing hot water with vomit and sometimes fecal matter, then throwing it at them. Between 1988 and 1990, their behavior had become so vicious that guards were forced to wear flak jackets and carry shields just to feed them. In fact, the last murder said to have been committed at the prison took place in cell twenty. The victim was cornered in his cell by a man he considered a friend and stabbed repeatedly. By the time guards arrived, blood covered the floor of his cell and had begun flowing out into the hallway. Now cell twenty and the surrounding area is said to be among the most haunted areas in the prison.

Our next stop was an indoor recreation area that was used on days when the weather was too harsh for inmates to be outside. But before descending the few steps that led to a dark basement-like area, our tour guide informed us of its unusual nickname. "Inmates," she said, "used to call this place the sugar shack!"

It didn't take long to see why it was given such a strange name. The sugar shack resembles a very large basement, but each of the stone pillars used to support the ceiling are adorned with murals—murals like the word *love* surrounded by hearts and flowers, or a silly frog trying to catch flies. Our tour guide didn't need to say another word, but she did. "Back in the day, trustees were permitted one hour of unsupervised chaos in which the sugar shack became a den of violence and homosexual rape. It had gotten so out of hand that even guards knew to never go there alone. But when the governor of West Virginia heard what was going on, he put an immediate stop to it and ordered the doors welded shut. Although no murders or deaths are known to have taken place here, it's considered high on the list of paranormal hotspots."

When the guided tour finally ended, our group got together in the visitation area for pizza and a short film about the prison, but Jayne and I slipped away in secret. This way, we might have the undivided attention of any ghostly inhabitants we encountered, and after having seen what I believe was the shadow man, Jayne and I wanted the maintenance area to ourselves.

We sat alone in the darkness for a long time, but there were no signs of paranormal activity, just a careless bat who swooped down a little too close to my head. I scolded the damn thing, but he didn't seem to care what I had to say about the marital status of his parents. He just flew around a few more times, and then he was gone. But why was he there? Some people believe insects are attracted to any area with a high degree of paranormal activity. The electromagnetic energy that can be detected with an EMF meter will also disrupt the navigation system in flying insects and draw them near. But then again, I thought, there isn't anything unusual about a bat chasing mosquitoes. Jayne and I sat there in silence a while longer before I decided to try to provoke a response. "Come on, R. D.," I said, standing up. "Do something! Can you be seen on film?" I asked. I began taking pictures but with little hope of catching anything on film; it just seemed to me the maintenance area was inactive. Yet a few days later when the pictures I had taken were developed, a smoky white orb appeared floating near the floor where the body of R. D. was found.

Could this be all that remains of R. D.? Just an orb drifting about the maintenance area? Or perhaps the real ghost of R. D. was the shadow man I saw in the yard, and the orb is merely residual energy caught on film. This could explain why the orb I photographed was in the same spot where the body was found. Great emotional energy must have been released when the murder took place, and now like ball lightning or some other natural phenomenon, it drifts around the room and when caught on film is sometimes mistaken for a ghost. In any case, I believed the maintenance area to be completely inactive and suggested we visit the sugar shack next.

The sugar shack was just as dark as the maintenance area, but we were able to find a couple of chairs and make ourselves comfortable, and once again Jayne and I found ourselves alone in the dark. But this time, I could feel a kind of presence in the air; it was like a rubber band about to snap. I had no idea how accurate my analogy was until a loud crackling sound split the darkness. I jumped to my feet and began taking pictures in the direction the sound came from while Jayne grabbed her video camera. When I finished taking pictures, I used my EMF meter to scan the area, but the red flashing light and alarm went on and off again as if I were tracking something in motion. While I walked around the room with my EMF meter in hand, Jayne began to complain that her camera was going in and out of focus.

"Maybe there's something wrong with it," I said, but Jayne shook her head.

"No. I've never seen anything like this before." I stood next to her and looked at the camera screen, but the image I saw was normal. Then only moments later, I heard her yell, "There it is again!" This time the image was blurry, like someone had smeared petroleum jelly on the lens, and then just as suddenly, it was clear again.

"That is weird," I said, walking away.

But when my EMF meter went off, Jayne said, "It's back!" And I turned to see her camera pointing directly at me.

"It's between us," I said. "Whatever it is, it's between us!" When I walked back to where Jayne was standing, I decided to stay and watch the screen for a while. I could see something move in front of us, causing the picture to blur, and then I watched it move away. "Did you see that?" I asked.

"Yeah," Jayne said, smiling, "we got something!"

When the photos I had taken were developed, they revealed large balloon-like orbs that were transparent rather than smoky white like those I had photographed in the maintenance area, which may well have caused Jayne's camera to blur as they passed in front of her. Also, the pictures taken when we heard the loud crackling sound revealed streamers of light that resembled the bottom of a swimming pool on a sunny day. Could the crackling

Co sound we heard have been the result of hostile energy being suddenly released into the atmosphere, as spirits relived some brutal attack they once committed against another inmate?

It's impossible to know what it was we experienced that night; we could only sit and wait to see if anything else might happen, but nothing ever did, and after a considerable amount of time, we decided to take our investigation elsewhere.

By this time, the other ghost hunters had begun to make their rounds, staking out places of interest and using their own methods to gather evidence of the paranormal. But still Jayne and I were able to find ourselves alone on some unknown cell block. We stood before a long row of cells where we found what appeared to be showers. As I stepped forward to investigate, Jayne produced a tape recorder from her equipment bag and tried to get an EVP or what is sometimes referred to as electronic voice phenomenon. The pictures I took in this area showed nothing out of the ordinary, but on the tape recording, my wife made it was possible to hear the faint murmuring of voices. It's impossible to say whether or not the sounds were made by an intelligent entity, but I felt certain it was nothing more than residual energy. Afterward, we made our way back to the visitation area where the pizza party had taken place so we could rest and reorganize our equipment. While we were there, we met a couple who invited us upstairs to the gymnasium, where they said they heard the sound of someone walking and photographed a red orb that contained a skull-like face peering out from its center.

As the four of us sat on the floor of the gym, we never heard anyone walking, but twice we witnessed a small red light suddenly appear and then disappear. I aimed my camera in that direction and began taking pictures, but the orbs I got were not at all red. They were the same balloon-like orbs we had seen in the sugar shack.

After a little while longer, Jayne and I decided to call it a night and head back to the hotel.

Former inmates once believed the soul of a man who died in prison could never leave, and perhaps they were right. The West Virginia State Penitentiary closed its doors in 1995. The inmates are gone, and the hallways are dark, but all is not quiet there. Voices whisper from within the empty cells, and shadows come to life. It's a place where residual energy fills the air, and I strongly recommend a visit.

CHAPTER EIGHT

＊◆◆◆＊

THE DESECRATION

Leaning forward in my seat, I looked in each direction, but the intersection was vacant. I was sitting at the start of a long, winding country road where traffic was usually light, and at two thirty in the morning, I knew my path would be clear. The radio seemed to read my thoughts as it played a song with the lyrics, *jumping off the deck, throw it in to overdrive, and straight into the danger zone!* Smiling, I revved the engine a few more times before pressing down hard on the accelerator.

Thrust back into my seat, I could hear the four-barrel carburetor sucking air as the Trans Am leapt forward. With its engine winding out, the surrounding landscape passed by at a hectic rate. Up and down hills and around every curve, its tires held the road like the paws of a large, black cat. As I reached the crest of a long, downward-sloping hill, I became momentarily weightless, and then as the song suggested, I threw it into overdrive! The car burst forward, almost flying along its downward course, but something would slow me down. Something always did.

Just up ahead, caught in the glare of my headlights, were the stone markers that seemed to peer up at me from behind the wrought-iron fence of a little cemetery. I took my foot off the accelerator and applied the brake until the car came to a stop.

There it was, a little graveyard hidden among the trees. Like grasping claws, their branches reached outward as if to reclaim the restless dead while, caught in autumn's chilly breath, their fallen leaves danced a minuet. And from somewhere among the lonely stones, a voice seemed to call out to me, "Don't go. Come sit with me a while and hear my tales of woe."

Years later while returning home from an afternoon fishing trip, I found myself once again driving down that same long and winding country road. But it was different now; the heavily wooded area had since been developed and was dotted with luxury homes. However, the little cemetery remained unchanged. Nestled quietly among the trees, it peered out from behind the wrought-iron fence that encircled it, and as I drove past, I could still feel the energy coming from within. But this time I understood what it was that seemed to call out to me, and this time I decided to stay awhile! And so pulling into the first driveway I came to, I turned around and headed back to the cemetery.

The evening air was calm and cool, and the setting park-like, but I couldn't shake the feeling of being watched as I walked slowly through the graveyard, reading the names of those who had been laid to rest there. Some of the headstones I found were old and broken down while others were simply illegible, but on some I could make out dates from as far back as the Revolutionary War. I continued walking along but hadn't yet made it to the center of the cemetery when the energy I once felt peering out at me as I drove past now seemed to stare directly at me! Like a sudden gust of wind, it came rushing toward me, stopping only a few feet away. It stood there demanding an answer to its only question: *who are you?* My blood ran cold, and my skin began to crawl as that same feeling of energy began to fill the air around me. I was completely surrounded by it. Now the cemetery was a dark and frightening place where the eyes of an unseen presence bore down on me.

"I know you're there," I said, looking around, but no response ever came. Instead, it began to fade away, and without my camera or any other equipment, I could do little more than go back to my car, excited by what I had found.

The following weekend, I went on another fishing trip, and this time I made sure to bring my camera, but as I stood at the water's edge watching my lure make its way back to me, I found myself more concerned with what I might get on film than with my next cast. I knew from experience there was something of a paranormal nature lingering there in the little cemetery. Even from the safety of my car, I could feel a presence as I drove past, and when I stopped to investigate further, it didn't hesitate to make itself known. Before long, anticipation got the better of me, and after putting my pole and tackle box in the car, I headed for the graveyard.

Streaks of amber and fire red crossed the sky as the evening sun began to set, and just as before, the air was cool and still, but the feeling of a presence was gone. Now only the chatter of birds filled the air around me, and that's when I remembered that the last time I was there it was quiet. There were no birds or insects, and not even the chirp of a single cricket disturbed the placid atmosphere. With this in mind, I walked slowly toward the middle of the cemetery, taking pictures at random. "Are you still here?" I asked. "Can you be seen on film?" I took picture after picture, and when I had exhausted an entire roll of film, I loaded another and began taking pictures again. When I neared the end of the second roll, I started walking back to my car, but something made me stop. I turned around and stood there for a moment. I looked around the cemetery and asked, "Will you let me have one good picture? Will you pose for the camera?" After using up the last of my film on the two headstones that stood in front of me, I headed for home.

When the film was developed, only the last two pictures I took revealed anything of interest. In the first one, an orb could be seen hovering high in the trees near where the road passes by, but in the second, a giant orb filled the center of the photograph just as if it had deliberately posed for the shot!

When my daughter, Samantha, saw the pictures I had taken, she smiled wide. "I'd love to get a few pictures like that," she said.

"Sure, why not. We can take my tape recorder with us and try for an EVP as well."

Sam was understandably excited; it would be her second time on a ghost hunt, and what better place to go than a haunted graveyard! It didn't take long before we were able to go, and soon we were at the cemetery taking pictures in every direction. When my film was developed, I had only one picture where I found something of interest. I had captured a light anomaly hovering just above a nearby row of headstones.

Oddly though, every picture my daughter took was completely black! It came as little consolation when I told her that in a way she did get something. "Why would your pictures come out black?" I asked. "It wasn't that dark, and your camera's flash was just as bright as mine. Maybe something prevented your camera from working!" I could tell she still felt a bit cheated, but she seemed a little more excited when I played back the tape recording of our ghost hunt.

At one point during our attempt at an EVP, Samantha asked, "Can you tell us your name?" And in a barely audible voice, we heard a response; it sounded like the name Jane!

That evening, our ghost hunt was the topic of discussion, and my wife came up with a great idea. "Maybe we should go back there," she said, "but this time we'll bring my divining rods!" It turned out to be an idea that would make this investigation one of the most intriguing of all.

The following weekend, Jayne and I went back to the cemetery, but we had gotten off to a late start and found ourselves in a race against time. "It's starting to get dark, and we still have a long way to go," I told her.

"Did you bring a flashlight?"

"No," I said. "I brought my camera and tape recorder, but I didn't think we would need a flashlight."

Jayne just shrugged. "Well, let's see what we can do tonight, and if we have to, we can always come back tomorrow."

When we finally arrived at the cemetery, the light of day had degraded to a dull gray, and so Jayne and I didn't waste any time getting started. Holding the rods out in front of herself, Jayne said, "If anyone here would like to communicate with us, please cross the rods to indicate yes or spread them apart if you wish to say no." Immediately the rods crossed and then spread apart, as if to say, *I understand.* Jayne's first question was "Are you a man?" And the rods widened—no. "Are you a lady?" Without hesitation, the rods crossed—yes! "Your ghost is a woman," Jayne said.

"What about a name?" I asked.

"If you tell us your name, we might be able to find your grave." Even before my wife could ask the question, the rods crossed again.

Using the alphabet, Jayne was able to spell out a woman's name, a name that sounded very similar to what Sam and I heard when we played back the tape recording of our own investigation, but by this time it was much too dark to stumble from headstone to headstone looking for the right one. "Well, at least we have a name, so maybe we can come back tomorrow and look for it," I said.

"Wait a minute," Jayne said. "Let me try something. Can you point us in the direction of your grave?" Her divining rods turned to the left, and Jayne followed with me right behind. Moving between and around the varied headstones, we ultimately made a large arc that led us back toward the road. Then suddenly the rods crossed, and Jayne stopped.

"This must be it," she said. "This is her grave!"

I bent down to read the name on the small, flat stone, but there wasn't one. Instead, it simply read *removed from cemetery 1943.*

At first I thought the rods had failed to lead us in the right direction. Removed from cemetery? "It just says removed from cemetery," I told Jayne. Then a startling wave of understanding washed over me as the puzzle pieces fell into place. "That's why she haunts! They moved her grave," I said, looking up at my wife.

After a little more effort, Jayne and I were able to get an answer as to why the body had been moved. It seems her biological family felt it would be better if it were taken to a cemetery where she would be surrounded by people of her own faith. However, the spirit was not so easily moved. Left behind, her ghost still roams the little cemetery, bemoaning the desecration of her final resting place. But when asked, "Will you ever move on and find peace?" an answer came quickly: yes!

CHAPTER NINE

THEY SAID SHE WASN'T WELL

The weather report called for a winter storm, and clouds had begun to accumulate, but the temperature was at least forty degrees, and I just didn't believe one was coming. "I don't think we have anything to worry about," I said, looking over at my wife. "They always predict these terrible overnight storms, but when you wake up the next day, it turns out to have been nothing more than a light dusting." Jayne, however, continued scanning the sky, and I could tell she took the weather man's warning a bit more seriously. "It'll be okay," I said. "If it's going to snow, it hasn't even started yet, and when it does, we'll probably be well out of harm's way." Jayne sat back in her seat and seemed a little more relaxed, so I suggested we stop and get a couple of energy drinks for that night's ghost hunt.

We had only been in the store long enough to pick up a few last-minute items, and in that short time, the temperature had dropped several degrees. As we walked across the parking lot, I watched a single snowflake glide gently to the ground. It was the first of a massive invasion, and even before we had gotten on the freeway, the snow was coming down hard and starting to pile up.

South of Cleveland, the roads were white, and even a simple lane change seemed like a daredevil feat, but as we approached Akron, conditions had gotten much worse. In front of me, brake lights flashed red, and I could feel the car begin to slide as my tires locked up on the icy road. "Do you think it's foolish to keep going?" Jayne asked.

But I thought it would be even more foolish to turn back. "After all," I said, "we're at least halfway through the storm, and if we turn back now, we'll have just as far to go only to end up at home." Fortunately, this time I was right, and only a short distance from Canton, things began to look a little better, but the hazardous driving conditions had put us far behind schedule, and now it was getting dark.

Though the storm lost its icy grip and the snow had become a slushy rain, the darkness made me feel uneasy as the unfamiliar roads of southeastern Ohio began to unfold. Jayne reached up and, turning on the dome light, she began searching for our location on the map. "How much further?" I asked.

"Not much," Jayne replied. Holding up the map, she pointed to the little town of Dresden and then to our position on the map. "Just keep your eyes open for the next exit; it shouldn't be long after that." Just as my wife had promised, it didn't take long before we found Prospect Place, a twenty-nine-room mansion that was built in 1856 by abolitionist George Wilson Adams.

The entire house was alive with history and a strong sense of the past. Even as we passed between the pillars that once made up the front gate, I could imagine the horses, wagons, and buggies that once made their way up the long, narrow driveway toward the house. But what stood out most of all was the barn.

It jumped out at me with a strong sense of presence. Watching me with its large, black eyes, it might have been described as spooky, eerie, or any other word that would indicate a ghostly presence. But suddenly the atmosphere changed to one of glee and arrogance, and I'm certain if the spirits inside could speak out loud, they would have asked with a smirk, "Did ya come to see some ghosts? Well come on in, boy, 'cause this is where we keep 'em." "You feel that?" I asked my wife, shrugging one shoulder in the direction of the old building.

Jayne shuddered as she looked back at me. "Yeah, I feel it." Before we made it to the door, I stopped and pointed out that all the other cars had snow on the windshields, so they probably belonged to the people who worked there. "That means no one else has come yet," Jayne said in an uneasy tone.

"Yeah, wouldn't it be great if we were here alone tonight?"

After looking at me as though I had lost my mind, Jayne followed me into the house. There was no one in sight. "Hello? Hello?" Jayne called out, but nobody answered. Then, leaning slightly forward as though she were able to send her voice out to find someone she tried again. "Hello? Hello?"

Moments later, a man appeared standing in the doorway. The young man who greeted us smiled broadly. "Here for the ghost hunt?" Jayne returned his smile and nodded.

"Are we the only ones here?" I asked.

"So far," he replied. "A couple of people called to say they wouldn't come because of the weather, so I'm sure other people are going to cancel as well." A feeling of excitement began to grow as I tried to imagine what it might be like to have the entire house to ourselves. No distractions, no interruptions, nothing to come between us and the restless shadows that whisper and moan. I could almost hear the chains begin to rattle when, as luck would have it, a pair of headlights came crawling slowly up the driveway.

"Looks like we'll have company after all," I said. Fortunately the two young ladies who would be our only companions for the night were a pleasant sort, and the old mansion offered plenty of room for all of us.

After the guided tour, Jayne and I wandered at random throughout the old house, trying to absorb the atmosphere, but we never did encounter anything of a malevolent nature. Instead, the energy I felt was that of quiet grace and dignity. The old house had once belonged to people of wealth and stature, and I realized then that unlike Mansfield Reformatory or the West Virginia State Penitentiary, any paranormal activity we might encounter would probably be more subtle and reserved. After spending some time exploring the lower floor, we ascended the staircase that led to the attic ballroom.

The ballroom was of course used for social gatherings, parties, and other events, but in a darker time when the house sat empty, it's believed that someone broke in, and the attic became a place of satanic worship. Claims of paranormal activity in this area include voices, children laughing, even the sound of a puppy scampering across the floor. One paranormal investigator who believed he could hear the puppy tried calling it but heard a man's voice call it back. Even our tour guide had a story to tell. I only felt intimidated once she went on to say, "And that was here in the ballroom." She pointed to one corner of the room and told us that she and her sister were sitting there in the dark listening for the sound of voices or perhaps the children who are said to play up there, but a new sound broke the silence. It was the sound of something growling. It sounded like a fierce dog, she said, but there was no dog!

Jayne and I felt nothing of a paranormal nature, and after sitting alone in the dark for quite some time, my wife decided to use her divining rods in an attempt at making contact with whoever or whatever haunts the ballroom.

"Is there anyone here with us tonight? Is there anyone here who would like to talk to us?" Jayne continued her attempt at making contact, but the rods remained still.

"Maybe we should try the tape recorder. After all, an animal spirit won't understand your questions."

"You got a point there," she said, sounding a bit amused. But our attempts at an EVP also failed, and in the end, even our pictures revealed nothing more than an empty room.

Jayne and I knew better than to be discouraged by the lack of activity in the attic. Every paranormal occurrence takes place on its own terms; all we can do is wait, watch, and listen. If the spirits want to get through, sooner or later they'll find a way, and with this in mind, we continued to explore the rest of the house. Our next stop was the basement. Because the basement is below ground level, the temperature is usually cooler than the rest of the house, making it an ideal place to store food, but it also has a darker history. Nearby, a passenger train unable to stop collided with a freight train that had somehow found its way onto the wrong track. The end result was twisted metal, fire, and death, but those who survived were brought to the basement where hopefully the cooler temperature might ease the pain suffered by the many burn victims, and people who are sensitive to the residual energy left behind can sometimes hear the moaning and wailing of those who suffered and died here. But there's yet another tragedy connected to the basement.

This is the story of Constance and her mother's unbearable grief. According to the tour guide, they said she wasn't well and probably delirious with fever when she stepped out on the second-floor balcony, where she slipped on the ice and fell to her death.

Unfortunately, the ground was too frozen to dig, and her body had to be kept in the basement until spring when she could be given a proper funeral. It's also said that her mother would sit for hours grieving over her daughter's lifeless body until she herself fell ill with a fever and died.

As I stood in the area where Constance had been laid out, I began taking pictures while my wife used her divining rods to speak with anyone who might be listening. When my film was developed, the pictures I had taken revealed nothing, but my wife had gotten a response that left us both puzzled, to say the least.

Jayne never prepared a list of questions but instead spoke in a casual manner as if making small talk, and tonight was no different. Holding the rods out in front of her, she politely asked, "Mrs. Adams, are you here with us tonight?" But the rods remained still. "Is there anyone here who would like to talk with us?" Now the rods began to waver in a back and forth motion as though someone who was perhaps shy and uncertain had made contact, and then slowly they crossed. "Constance, is that you?" Jayne asked. And without hesitation, they crossed again.

"This is a very beautiful house," Jayne said. "Did you enjoy living here?" This time the rods did something I've never seen them do before; they crossed only at the very ends and then widened and crossed again. Watching this, I felt a sense of uncertainty; it was as if the spirit didn't know how to answer the question. "I heard about your illness," Jayne said. "Is that why you fell from the balcony?" Suddenly the rods shot forward into the neutral position, and this time her response was clear: *I don't want to talk about this!* Jayne tried several more times to re-establish contact, but it was useless. Constance was gone.

After searching around in the darkness, we found a couple of chairs at the other end of the basement and decided to stay awhile longer. Though Constance would no longer speak with us, the basement is believed to be haunted by the many tragic souls who perished as a result of the nearby train crash, and perhaps tonight one of them would make contact with us.

Jayne and I sat patiently waiting for any sign of the paranormal, and then at last something happened. An icy-cold breath of air gently caressed the back of my neck. But I didn't say anything about it to my wife. Instead, I waited to see if it would happen again, and moments later it did. The temperature around me seemed to drop several degrees in just a few short minutes, and I believe what I experienced that night may have been something commonly referred to as a "cold spot." But considering the weather outside, it could have been nothing more than a cold draft in a very old house, and so I continued to sit quietly beside my wife. Eventually she began to complain about the same drop in temperature I had been feeling, and I just didn't see any reason to stay. The basement was cold, and I had no sense of any paranormal energy.

We were warmer now that we had made our way back upstairs, but the atmosphere was completely different. The basement may have been the scene of great tragedy, but up in the rest of the house, this was where they lived their lives, and I could feel that all around me. It was as if they were still there, existing in an unseen world where they continued to live just as they once did.

Jayne led the way, and I followed right behind her until we had come full circle and found ourselves where the tour had first begun. This was the gentlemen's room, our guide had said. It was where Mr. Adams would meet with the other men from town and discuss business and politics. As I sat down on the couch, I remembered how our guide smiled when she looked at my wife and the other two girls who had also come for the ghost hunt. "There were no women allowed in this room, not in his day," she said, pointing at a picture that hung above the fireplace.

So that's George Adams, I thought, looking up at the painting of a man dressed in black. His eyes were piercing and filled with anger as he looked back at me, and I knew with one look this was his house, he built it, and things would be done his way.

Turning my attention away from the painting, I looked at my wife, who was standing directly in front of the fireplace, holding her divining rods out in front of her. "George Adams, are you here with us tonight?" Again she asked, "George Adams, are you here with us tonight?" Still the rods didn't move or even waver in the least. "Is there anyone here who would like to talk with us?" The rods remained motionless.

"Let me try," I said. Taking the rods from my wife, I held them out and asked, "Mr. Adams, are you here?" The rods quickly responded yes. "Will you talk with me?" Again they responded yes. "Why won't you talk with my wife? Is it because she's a woman?" *Yes*. "Do you want her to leave?" *Yes*. Laughing, I handed the rods back to my wife. "This is the gentlemen's room," I said, "and you're not supposed to be here." My wife looked back at me with an expression of bewilderment, but I was just as puzzled by her reaction. *What's so hard to understand? I wondered quietly. It's the gentlemen's room; that means no women allowed!*

Once again, Jayne and I began wandering the first floor, but we hadn't gotten very far when we came to the room that was once used by Mrs. Adams. Just as Mr. Adams had the gentlemen's room, Mrs. Adams had a room where she and the ladies from town would gather together, and it was here that a terrible secret would be revealed. Expecting to make contact with the spirit of Mrs. Adams, my wife held out her divining rods and asked, "Mrs. Adams, are you here?" When the rods failed to give a response, my wife tried again, but still they continued to point forward. "Is there anybody else who would like to talk with us?" Slowly they crossed—yes! "Constance, is that you?" my wife asked. But the rods widened, no. "Mr. Adams?" Then with a quick and purposeful motion, the rods crossed, yes. Jayne glanced up at me with a nervous expression. "He's been following us," she said. But with a shrug of her shoulders, she continued to question George Adams in the same casual manner she had used before.

"How many children did you have?" My wife began counting, "One, two," and when she had finally reached seven, they suddenly crossed. "Seven? You had seven children?" Her rods crossed again, yes. "I'm sorry to hear about your daughter Constance. I heard she was very ill when she went out on the balcony. Is that why she fell?" Suddenly, just as they had done in the basement, the rods began to waver, crossing and uncrossing, yes, no, yes, no. Jayne looked up at me and, frowning, asked, "What does that mean?"

The answer to her question hit me like a ton of bricks. "Ask him if she jumped!" But before she could get the words out of her mouth, the rods crossed and then returned to the forward position where they refused to move again. George Adams was gone!

Later that evening, Jayne and I found ourselves once again sitting quietly in the gentlemen's room, but as I sat there looking up at the portrait of Mr. Adams, I began to wonder why the subject of his daughter's death was such a sensitive topic. In the 1800s, people had a limited understanding of mental illness, and her condition may have been considered an embarrassment. I could also imagine how family members would have been deliberately vague when asked what happened. "She wasn't well," they would say, misleading people into believing she had come down with a fever and her suicide was a tragic accident. Even though a fall from such a height would certainly cause serious injury, it may not have been the cause of her death. We would later be told that county records indicate she died of tuberculosis, and realizing my suspicions were nothing more than a fantasy, I put the notion out of my head. But still I had to wonder why the rods behaved the way they did.

Soon we heard the sound of footsteps as they echoed down the hall, and moments later the two young ladies we met earlier that evening entered the room. The four of us sat quietly for only a short time before introducing ourselves. "Have you had any luck?" I asked. They told us they had spent most of their time in the attic ballroom but with little success. "We didn't do any good up there either," Jayne said, but then she told them about her divining rods and how she made contact with George Adams and his daughter Constance. After that, our conversation turned to the history of the house, but in the end we all agreed the barn would be a good place to visit next.

According to local legend, a bounty hunter came to the Adams' house and accused Mr. Adams of taking part in the Underground Railroad, in which runaway slaves were smuggled across the border into Canada. Irate, the bounty hunter drew his gun and demanded that any slaves he had been hiding be turned over immediately.

But George Adams was not so easily intimidated. He drew his own weapon, and the two men stood toe to toe until nearby farm hands came to the aid of their employer. Outmanned and outgunned, the bounty hunter had no choice but to leave the property and never return. However, a psychic who visited Prospect Place claims the story didn't end there. Fearful he might return and kill their employer, the farm hands went out that night in search of the bounty hunter. After finding him, they brought him back to the barn where he was put on trial for crimes against humanity and hanged. Now his ghost dwells among the rafters where his life came to an end, and with our two new friends following close behind, we headed for the barn in hopes of finding him. I was disappointed by the lack of space on the first floor, but Jayne had enough room to use her divining rods, and with them in hand, she called out to the bounty hunter, "Are you here?" No response came, so she tried again, but still there was no answer.

"Maybe we need to be on the second floor," I suggested. "Remember, the tour guide said they took him up there when they hung him, and I'll bet he fell through there," I said, pointing to a large square opening in the ceiling. Right in front of us there was a narrow stairway leading to the second floor, but it was closed off due to disrepair, and we were forced to stay on the landing.

This time, when my wife held out the rods and called out to the ghost of the bounty hunter, the rods crossed, and Jayne smiled as she looked back at the three of us. "We found him!"

Jayne began her line of questioning by asking, "Are you trapped here?" The rods crossed, yes. "Will you ever leave?" *No.* When she asked, "Do you know what year it is?" the rods would only waver back and forth as though confused by the question. "This is 2007. Did you know that?" Again the rods began to waver back and forth, and Jayne looked back at us, shaking her head. "I don't think he knows how long he's been here." Then she asked, "Are you sorry for what you did?" And the answer came back without hesitation or uncertainty, no.

Standing there, I remembered what our tour guide said about the bounty hunter's willingness to interact and communicate, so I asked, "Will you do something to prove you're really here?" Suddenly a scraping sound could be heard coming from somewhere on the second floor. "Did you guys hear that?" I asked, looking back at the others. Everyone agreed they heard something, so I asked, "Will you do it again?" Seconds later, the sound came again, and just as before it was impossible to tell where it came from or what might have made it!

When we left the barn, there didn't seem to be any doubt as to whether or not it was haunted, but for me the question remained—by whom? Though by today's standards the bounty hunter would be considered an evil man, in the days prior to the Civil War, attitudes were vastly different. The bounty hunter may have felt he had a right to earn a living in this manner and the actions taken against him were nothing less than a murder. So why is the ghost of a murdered man who's been trapped in the darkness of an old barn for more than one hundred years so compliant?

I also had to wonder why the farm hands that went out in search of the bounty hunter didn't kill him as planned, but instead brought him back to the barn where he was put on trial and then executed for completely different reasons. I can only assume George Adams had no knowledge of what his men did that night, but the barn stands only a few yards from the house where he lived, and yet they seemed to have no fear of being caught. Could

George Adams have been more involved than anyone ever knew? Or perhaps the psychic was simply wrong and the bounty hunter never died there at all. I only know when Jayne and I first arrived at Prospect Place, we both felt a presence coming from inside the barn. But the photos I took that night reveal multiple orbs and light anomalies, which leads me to believe the barn is haunted by several entities, not just one. And as I looked back at the old building, I was forced to wonder if it wasn't the farm hands themselves watching us as we walked away.

After our visit to the barn, the four of us went to the dining room where we sat for a while drinking coffee and talking about what we had just experienced. This was their first ghost hunt, and our two companions were very interested in Jayne's divining rods. The one girl in particular seemed the most interested, asking, "Where did you get them? Will they work for anyone?"

Before I could finish my coffee, we were on our way to the basement where Jayne had promised her she could try them for herself. Holding the rods out in front of her as Jayne instructed, she asked, "Is there anyone here who would like to talk to us?" She smiled with a look of disbelief as the rods crossed, yes! Then believing she might be in contact with Constance she asked, "What is your name?" Jayne explained to her how she could use the alphabet to get an answer, but when she tried, the name that came back was Dennis. "Are you a member of the Adams family?"

Suddenly from somewhere in the darkness, a voice broke the silence, "Na na na nut." Laughter ensued as we recognized it as the theme from that old TV show, *The Adams Family*.

But a more serious attitude prevailed when the rods crossed, and we learned that he was the second cousin of Mary Adams. "Why did you die? Were you sick?" The answer to her question came quickly, yes! "Was it pneumonia?" *No!*

My wife interrupted the conversation. "Ask him if it was tuberculosis." When she did, the rods crossed, yes!

The next line of questioning concerned whether or not there were any photographs of Dennis in the house, and the response that came back was yes. "Will you follow us upstairs and help us find the right picture?" Again he responded by crossing the rods, and soon the four of us were standing in front of a large glass case that housed artifacts that had been found while renovating the house. After making sure that Dennis had come with us, my wife began pointing to the different people who appeared in the photographs. At first the rods widened, no, no, no, and then suddenly at the very end, the rods crossed, yes! "That's him," Jayne said, pointing to the likeness of a young boy. The girls were astonished by the success we had in communicating with what appeared to be the ghost of a young man named Dennis, and as they talked among themselves, I stood quietly, my head spinning in disbelief.

I've always considered the divining rods to be nothing more than unscientific hocus pocus, but at the same time I've never been able to explain how they work, and tonight even in the hands of a stranger they identified family members, answered questions, and pointed out the likeness of a young man named Dennis. As these events began to unfold, I found it harder and harder to believe my eyes, and I had to wonder, could any of this be real?

Skeptics are quick to blame the user by saying it was all done subconsciously, but that explanation seems a little too convenient. Like a magic word, it's a blanket explanation for anything the skeptic isn't ready to accept, and with no way to prove otherwise, he'll seem scientific and knowledgeable. But is there any way to prove the rods really were influenced by the subconscious? Truth is, bullshit works both ways, and I can only say, what happened, happened and what I saw, I saw.

In the morning when it was time to leave, we encountered our tour guide from the night before and told her about some of the things that had happened to us. She laughed a little when we told her about the scraping sound we heard in the barn and then reminded us how willing the bounty hunter is to communicate. But when we began talking about Constance, and she told us that Constance wasn't actually the biological daughter of Mr. and Mrs. Adams. She was in fact adopted into the Adams' family as a child, and though she died at the age of twenty, she often appears to women as a smiling fourteen-year-old girl. I began to imagine how her early teenage years may have been the only truly happy time in her life and how that might explain why she appears to people at that age. But what happened to her as an adult?

Did Constance die quietly in her bed from an illness known as consumption or is there a darker secret? Before walking out the door, I was for some reason compelled to stop and tell our tour guide everything the rods had said; according to them, she didn't fall, she jumped! Her eyes widened as she gasped, and then she shuddered as though a cold wind had sliced right through her. "I'll have to tell someone about this," she said. Judging from her reaction, it would seem my comment had struck a nerve, but why?

As I stepped outside and closed the door behind me, sealing in whatever dark secrets, tragedies, or mysteries that might remain, only one thought echoed through my head. *"Did ya come to see some ghosts? Well come on in 'cause this is where we keep 'em!"*

CHAPTER TEN
A MESSAGE LEFT BEHIND

One look at the Cashtown Inn and I knew it had been a part of the landscape for many years, and for those who had seen the movie *Gettysburg,* it was an icon of historical significance.

The Cashtown was built in the late 1700s, but it also served as headquarters for General A. P. Hill during the Battle of Gettysburg, and although its atmosphere is warm and charming, some will say it harbors the memory of war and the souls of those who perished in battle. Visitors sometimes claim to hear unusual sounds in the night, sounds like that of a man in boots walking across the room. And on occasion, the smell of cigar smoke lingers in the air while out front the porch swing begins to sway though the night is still and windless.

Some have even been fortunate enough to catch a glimpse of the Confederate soldier who stands in the hallway looking in every direction as though searching for someone. He then disappears through a closed door, leaving no further trace of his whereabouts. No one has ever described the apparition as frightening, but nonetheless, it's an experience any ghost hunter would love to have. As for the room we would be staying in, Jayne and I had specifically requested number four. Room number four was warm and sunny, but like the rest of the inn, it held a strong sense of history and a reputation for paranormal activity. My wife began to unpack and settle herself into the room while I sat quietly in a chair next to the window.

I began to imagine what the view might have been like early in the summer of 1863. As the highway out front transformed into a simple dirt road, I could hear the clamor of heavy artillery and the wagons loaded with ammunition drawing near. Then came the sound of men; by the thousands, they came steadily marching toward me, their bayonets glistening in the sun as the endless line of gray made its way past.

Soon the air would be filled with the smell of smoke and the sound of fighting, but it was the drone of a lawn mower that shattered my illusion, and the shards of fantasy fell away as I awoke from my daydream. Turning in my chair, I found my wife sitting on the bed, her head tilted slightly as she smiled and asked, "Ya back?" Jayne knew how much I enjoyed our trips to Gettysburg, and I returned her smile as I stood up, fishing through my pockets for the car keys.

"I guess you want lunch, right?" But before leaving, I set the same trap I used at the Farnsworth House. Unfortunately though, in my haste I had forgotten to leave an EMF meter near the tape recorder, and without it, there would be much less evidence that anything caught on tape was of a paranormal nature. But at least the recorder was set, and with a little luck it would give a chilling account of any events that took place in our absence.

After lunch, Jayne and I made our way through town, stopping at the various antique shops to study the many odds and ends that time had left behind. It seemed that this could be the start of a brand-new hobby for us as we searched the stores along Baltimore Street hoping to find that one particular object that would beam out at us, telling us of its previous owner and the trauma that followed him through life. But without psychic ability, our quest was a hopeless one, although it did provide us with an entertaining afternoon. Soon though, it was time to head back to the inn, where we had been invited to have dinner with a local psychic.

The dinner was one that any chef would be proud of, but it was the psychic that took the spotlight. The people in attendance were amazed as she told us who we were and what we had been doing with our lives, giving each of us details she couldn't have known. In some cases, however charlatans, and so-called psychics will use an age-old trick; they simply ask questions that are intentionally vague. For example, does the month of May mean anything to you? Suddenly it's your responsibility to think of a reason why that month is important, and if you can't, it will seem as though you're to blame. The psychic will then move quickly from question to question, letting you fill in the blanks, making it appear as though the information was attained by means of psychic ability, when in reality every answer came directly from you. The trick is as simple as shooting an arrow in some random direction and then running up and drawing the target around it. Our psychic for the evening was quite different though; she never asked questions or used conversation to probe for answers. Instead she came to us one by one until finally she turned to me, encouraging me to continue working on the book while congratulating my wife on the purchase of her new car. I've always been skeptical of psychics and their professed ability, but Jayne and I sat in the corner of the dining room and had said nothing to anyone about the book or her new car. As the evening progressed, she began talking about the Battle of Gettysburg, saying that many of us are drawn here by past-life memories and the need to once again heed the call to arms. Incredible as it sounded, I had to think about the people who come to visit the battlefield. Every year they come by the thousands, and many will return year after year, gazing out onto an open field as if trying to remember something they never experienced.

By the time dinner was over, the sun had gone down, giving way to a moonless night. Already aware we had forgotten the battlefield map, we drove slowly, guessing at which direction we should take as the road began to narrow and wind through the rolling hills of the Pennsylvania state park. At times, our way seemed little more than a footpath as our headlights were cut short by the sudden turns and heavy woods that surrounded us. We came to crossroads only to be cheated out of our choice of direction by signs that would spring up, declaring one way or simply "do not enter."

Smiling to myself, I began thinking about the only battlefield story that truly upset my wife; it was a rumor told about the animals. During the Battle of Gettysburg, many local farms were set upon by the Confederate Army, and much of the livestock was displaced and set free to roam the countryside. Soldiers whispered stories back and forth about the hogs that had become carnivorous, feeding on the dead and sometimes, worse, the wounded! With this in mind, two young men sat along the roadside one summer night looking for signs of the paranormal when a spectral image appeared before them; there, staring in the window was the demonic face of a goat. *True or not, it's a good story*, I thought. Then suddenly there he was, the figure of a soldier stood by the side of the road as if waiting to march across. Caught in the glow of our headlights, the statue had come to life, and it seemed as if an entire regiment had begun to surround this familiar totem. Filling the woods around us, they watched from behind every tree as we drove slowly by. "What the hell was wrong with that statue?" I asked.

"I don't know," Jayne replied, "but for a second I thought the damn thing was going to turn its head and look right at me!" Soon we came to a sharp turn in the road.

"Where the hell are we?" I asked.

"I don't know," Jayne said, "but I think we're going in circles.

"Oh shit! We've got bigger problems now," I said, looking down at the gauges in front of me. "I forgot to get gas!"

"How low are we?"

"We have to get out of here right now," I said, "or we'll be walking the rest of the way." Jayne became quiet and perhaps a little frightened by the idea of walking through the woods at night. I had to find some way to console her, but as I looked over at her and her eyes locked onto mine, I could only think of one thing to say. "Hope that damn goat face don't show up!"

"Knock that shit off," Jayne snapped back at me, obviously unable to see the humor in what I had said. Soon the way out became apparent, and the tension began to ease up, but looking down at her lap, I saw she had been holding her cell phone.

"What were you going to do with that?" I asked

"Call 911," she said, "you know, in case we ran out of gas or something."

"And what were you going to say? 'Help, we're out of gas, and I think I saw a ghost'? Or, 'Help, help, the scary goat face is after me!'" By this time, we had found our way out of the park, and we both began to laugh. Not far from the park, we found an open gas station, and this time I made sure to fill the tank, but it was much later than either of us thought it was, and so we decided to call it a night.

When we got back to the inn, Jayne went immediately to the bathroom, and I sat down on the edge of the bed and kicked off my shoes. I was a little disappointed that our only battlefield experience was nothing more than what comes from an overactive imagination, but then I remembered something—the tape recorder! It was set on voice activation and had been running for several minutes while we were away. First came the sound of Jayne and I leaving the room, keys jingling, footsteps, the door closing, and so on. Next came the sound of a lawn mower, probably the one from before, I thought as I continued to listen. The sound of our neighbors came next, slamming doors and loud voices as they stomped down the hall like elephants, and I realized then that I had the recorder set to its most sensitive setting.

Another wave of disappointment washed over me when it occurred to me that at such a sensitive setting, the recorder had probably picked up every little sound that can be commonly heard in the room, and what I heard next was as ordinary as a barking dog and a motorcycle speeding past, but after that came something else on the tape, not like our neighbors in the hallway or the dog in the yard, and it was much closer. First came the thumping sound and then a long, drawn-out rumble. I rewound the tape only as far as necessary and listened again—thump, thump, thump, and then came the rumbling sound. When Jayne came out of the bathroom, I called her over. "Listen," I said as I rewound the tape. "Here—listen to this." The sounds came again just as they did before—thump, thump, thump, and then a long, drawn-out rumbling.

Jayne looked at me with a puzzled frown. "What was that?" she asked.

"I don't know," I said, "but at least we have something to think about." During the night, I woke up twice and peered cautiously around the room for anything of a paranormal nature, but the room was no more frightening in the dark than it had been all day long. There was no smell of cigar smoke or any sound of boots walking across the floor.

During breakfast, I fished around in my bag for the tape recorder and played the tape again. Thump, thump, thump, and then the rumbling sound. What the hell could it be? I wondered. The sound was like nothing I had ever heard before, and yet it was so familiar. While driving home, it seemed useless to play the tape again; whatever the sound was, it was simply unidentifiable. As for the statue, all humor had run out of the subject, but we did begin to wonder if we hadn't encountered something in the woods that night.

The energy that made the statue seem alive, and the presence in the woods around it was certainly strong and unsettling, but we had failed to obtain evidence of anything unusual, so our experience will never be anything more than personal. On the following day after we had gotten home, Jayne took our film to be developed, but nothing unusual came out on any of the pictures.

"That's too bad," I said, "but at least we had a good time, right?" Jayne smiled in agreement and then asked if I wanted coffee. As she got up and headed toward the kitchen, I looked down at the tape recorder I had left sitting on the table in front of me, and I couldn't help but listen one more time. Thump, thump, thump, and then came the rumbling sound. But even before I had a chance to wonder what could have made the sound, two words burst into my head—cigar smoke! I pushed fast forward and rolled the tape ahead so I wouldn't disturb anything I had already recorded. Then I pushed record, and with my index finger I tapped three times and blew lightly on the face of the recorder. The sound it produced was exactly the same as what I had recorded in our room. I thought about some of the notes and letters left behind by other guests of room four. Some claimed to have heard footsteps while others could smell cigar smoke, but there were also those who claimed the smell of smoke was blown directly in their face. When I played the tape back for Jayne, her eyes widened. He left a message!

CHAPTER ELEVEN

THREE HAUNTS OF THE BATTLEFIELD

During our many visits to Gettysburg, Jayne and I always chose to stay at a bed and breakfast or inn that was said to be haunted, and although the focus on my attention has been on such places, not every visit has provided us with a paranormal experience. In fact, on occasion, the only experience we had came from the battlefield itself, but what we found often seemed of little significance. However, I thought our experiences might still be of interest to the reader, and so I've decided to put these incidents together in a section of their own.

Shadows

On one particular evening, Jayne and I spent most of our time among the boulders that make up Devil's Den. But areas like Devil's Den and the Triangular Field are popular among tourists and ghost hunters alike, and soon Jayne and I were surrounded by people. Preferring to be alone, we began wandering the park at random, looking for a secluded spot where we could continue with our investigation. As we rolled slowly along, we passed other ghost hunters who had stopped on the side of the road to take pictures of the open field where Pickett's charge took place. It seemed like an excellent idea, but the flash from our simple cameras wouldn't be strong enough to reveal anything other than the surrounding darkness, and so we continued on our way, looking for an ideal spot, but nothing seemed to inspire either of us. "What about Spangler's Spring?" I said. "Not many people go there."

"Pull over so I can check the map," Jayne said, turning on the dome light. I watched my wife unfold the battlefield map and begin looking for Spangler's Spring, but from the corner of my eye, I could see a large, black shadow drifting back and forth in a field several yards away. As I looked up, its movement suddenly stopped. It was as if it had tried to conceal itself from me, and I knew I had glimpsed something strange, but now the only thing I could see was a shadow that seemed to blend in with the trees and surrounding darkness.

Again I looked down at the map Jayne was holding. "Can't you find it?" I asked.

"Hang on a minute," she said, and as she spoke, I saw the shadow move again. It was the size of a cow and shapeless like a giant, black garbage bag blowing in the wind. Its movements were erratic; it moved in a back-and-forth motion that was inconsistent with any normal wind pattern, and just as it had done before, when I looked up, its movement suddenly stopped, and it again began to melt into the surrounding darkness. But this time I noticed something—when the shadow stopped, it was in a different place!

I searched the area for anything that might cause a shadow of that size, but even with my high beams on, I couldn't find anything. I looked back at my wife, but this time when I looked down at the map she was holding, I kept my attention focused on the shadow, and I watched it emerge from the same spot where it had stopped before. Keeping my head down, I watched it as it danced defiantly in every direction, but when I lifted my head and looked directly at it, the shadow stopped where it was and faded away.

"Okay, I found it," Jayne announced. "Just go straight ahead." As we pulled away from the stop sign and crossed the street in front of us, I slowed down to a crawl and looked where I had seen the shadow only moments before, but it was gone now. "You saw that too, didn't you?"

"What did you see?" I asked.

Jayne shrugged. "It was like some kind of shadow or something," was all she said, and I wondered if we had really seen the same thing or not. Didn't she see it move back and forth and then stop moving altogether when she looked directly at it? And didn't she notice there was nothing in the surrounding area that would cast a shadow like that? I could only press down on the accelerator and drive away. Whatever it was, it was gone now, and by this time tomorrow, it would be hundreds of miles away.

Hungry Ghosts

On another occasion, Jayne and I had spent most of the evening in town, which left little time to explore the battlefield, and by the time we had gotten there, it was already getting dark. We drove slowly through the park, but nothing seemed to arouse a feeling of paranormal activity until we came across the same statue that had chilled us to the bone once before.

Carved in stone, it was the likeness of a Confederate soldier with his rifle at the ready. He looked as if he were about to march across the street right in front of us. The stone itself seemed to come alive as we passed, and the surrounding woods may well have been filled with the souls of men who had been lost in battle. But this time, the feeling of paranormal energy wasn't nearly as strong or frightening, and we were compelled to stop for a moment and take a picture of the statue, the statue we now refer to as our creepy little friend. We got out of the car and stood in the cool night air, taking pictures of the statue and surrounding woods, but our photographs revealed nothing other than trees and the darkness around us. "Here, how about this?" Jayne asked, handing me an EMF meter.

"I don't think it'll work tonight," I said. "There doesn't seem to be anything out here but squirrels, and they're probably all curled up with their nuts tucked in, wishing we would go away and let them sleep. But if you insist, I'll give it a shot." Walking over to the statue, I held out the EMF meter, but the device remained silent. "See? Told ya so," I said.

I had no idea how late it was when I asked her if she had any interest in getting dinner; I only knew I hadn't eaten for a long while and I was hungry.

"What did you have in mind?" Jayne asked.

"We saw a KFC in town, remember?" The idea sounded good to her too, so before getting in the car, I turned to scan the area one last time, and waving my hand in the air, I said, "Come on, all you hungry Confederate ghosts. Let's go get some good southern fried chicken!"

"I really wish you'd stop doing that," Jayne said. "They can hear you!"

"Well, if any of 'em show up, I'll buy 'em some chicken," I said, nodding my head in the fashion of Oliver Hardy.

After leaving the battlefield, it didn't take long to locate the restaurant, but the parking lot was empty, and the lights were dim. "Shit! It's closed," I said, and with that, the EMF meter in Jayne's lap began to scream, and its red warning light began flashing wildly. With her eyes wide and her body rigid, Jayne looked down at the EMF meter as though it were a big, hairy spider that had crawled up her leg. When she looked up at me, she didn't need to say a word. I knew exactly what she was thinking. Someone had come along for the ride!

Without a word, I turned into the parking lot and got out of the car. This had to be more than a coincidence, I thought as I took the first picture. Jayne's expression didn't change; she just sat there staring back at me until the alarm finally stopped, and then she began to relax a bit. "Someone was in the car with us!" she said. "I didn't see anybody," I said laughing, but when the pictures were developed, a strange light anomaly appeared in the passenger side window.

Was it a reflection from the dome light? Or maybe the camera's flash? Perhaps it came from some other unidentified source. I don't know. I only know there's something strange about the way it appears in the photograph, and looking at it makes me wonder, was there someone in the car with us? Did someone take my invitation seriously? I began to feel bad as I thought about the men who fought in our Civil War. At times, many of them got by on little more than hard tack and dried beef while others had only water. Maybe Jayne was right and I should watch what I say. Maybe they can hear me after all!

Man on the Bridge

There was another incident that took place in a lesser-known part of the battlefield, a place called Sachs Bridge, and on this particular trip to Gettysburg, our thirteen-year-old daughter, Samantha, had asked if she could come with us. After hearing our many stories of haunted houses and things that go bump in the night, she had become curious about the paranormal and was eager to have an experience of her own. Why not? I thought. Sometimes the world is a simple place where reality is black and white. But in the world of psychic phenomenon, I could show her what I've seen myself and let her sort through the many shades of gray, not only to determine what is and isn't real, but perhaps to deepen her sense of who and what we are.

It had taken sometime for Jayne and I to finish making plans and arrangements for the trip, but finally I was able to tell Sam that she was welcome to come. She raised her fist in the air and with one quick motion as if pulling on some invisible lever, she brought it down. "Yeah!" she said, her eyes filled with excitement. I tried to remind her that sometimes our ghost hunts were uneventful—in fact, *rather boring* was how I described it—but she didn't seem to care, and so I explained to her that there were also times when things did happen, things that would make her blood run cold! Her smile broadened into something devilish. "Awesome!"

"All right then. If you're so brave, I'll take you to Sachs Bridge."

"What's that?" she asked.

"It's a place most people don't know about," I told her. "Sachs Bridge was built in the 1850s, and at the end of the Battle of Gettysburg when the Confederate Army began its retreat from the battlefield, they had to cross it, but not before stopping long enough to execute three soldiers who were accused of desertion. They were three men, two from Virginia and one from Tennessee, and they say you can feel a cold spot on the bridge. That's where they were hanged! I also heard if you knock three times on the third rafter and shout, 'Virginia, Virginia, Tennessee!' something will happen."

"What?" Sam asked.

"I don't know. I just know the bridge is supposed to become active. Wanna try it?"

The look in her eyes became somewhat distant as though she were developing a mental picture of what might happen, but once again a smile crossed her face, and the devilish look returned. "Yeah, let's do it!"

Our drive to Gettysburg was long and slow, but finally we made it to town, where we spent a few hours before taking Sam to see Sachs Bridge. In the light of day, Sachs Bridge is a calm and picturesque place where the glassy waters of Marsh Creek reflect the serenity of nature while concealing a monstrous past, a past I didn't feel my daughter needed to know.

During the Battle of Gettysburg, it was used as a field hospital, a place where doctors made their way from man to man, sorting out the dead and dying from those who were worth trying to save. It was a place where doctors did what had to be done. They kept their hearts hard and their ears closed to the sounds of men as they cried out in pain and begged for the cutting to stop, but their only reply was the sound of a bone saw.

Ringlets appeared on the surface of the calm green waters below as blood dripped from between the floor boards of Sachs Bridge, and the amputations continued. Some would eventually find their way home again, home to their family farms and the open arms of their sweethearts, but for many, Sachs Bridge was nothing more than a place out of the sun, a place where they could die in the shade.

"Well, there it is," Jayne said. "There's your bridge."

Samantha was already leaning forward in her seat, gazing out the window, and I could tell she was impressed by its placid beauty. "It looks nice," she said, "not spooky at all."

I had to admit that in the light of day I myself had been distracted by thoughts of fishing and relaxing on the bank. "It's a whole different place at night," I warned her. "In fact, I'll bet you don't have nerve enough to walk across the bridge by yourself." Samantha smiled and began her leisurely stroll across the bridge, stopping only to read the graffiti left behind by local teenagers. When she returned, Sam seemed happy to report that Sachs Bridge was no different from any other bridge. "Yeah? Bet you won't have nerve enough to do that tonight."

After the sun went down, we made our way back out to the battlefield where we introduced Samantha to our "creepy little friend." The statue stood in the glow of our headlights, and much as before, a presence seemed to gather among the surrounding trees, watching us, waiting for a chance to approach.

As we drove into the night, it seemed the entire battlefield was alive with the same oppressive energy. By this time, the hour had become late, and the tourists had gone to town where they would commence their invasion of the souvenir shops, bars, and restaurants, leaving us alone among the stones of Devil's Den. In the darkness, I found a name carved into the rock, the name P. Noel. Locals will say the name was carved by some long-ago park maintenance worker, but others will say it was done by the ghost of Pauline Noel, a young girl who had been decapitated in a horrible carriage accident. According to legend, if you trace the letters with your finger, the headless ghost of Pauline Noel will appear!

I never believed the legend of Pauline Noel, and for me the letters were obviously carved with hammer and chisel. But then again, there's only one way to know for sure, so without hesitation, I leaned over, and with my index finger I traced the letters. Did the ghost of Pauline Noel show up? Of course not! Tracing the letters only made me feel stupid, but for those who have kids, it's a good story that comes with a chilling dare! Afterward, I searched around in the darkness until I found my wife and daughter. Jayne was troubled by something, something she couldn't explain. "I don't think we should be here," she said. "I feel like we're being watched!" Samantha seemed to share her mother's feelings of dread, but for me their fear was encouraging.

"Maybe we're not alone," I suggested. I began taking pictures in every direction, hoping to catch something on film, but Jayne and Sam became increasingly nervous.

"Come on, let's go," Jayne insisted.

"Not yet—just a little longer, okay?" I continued taking pictures until I heard Jayne's voice calling me. But this time, she sounded frightened.

"There's something moving around down there by our car!" Peering through the darkness I could see exactly what it was, and I laughed.

"It's a cat," I said. I continued taking pictures, but Jayne became increasingly more agitated.

"It's still down there," she said.

"So? It's just a cat!"

My wife was on the verge of panic when she took our daughter by the hand and hurried back to the car. She left in such haste I was concerned for their safety as they made their way through the darkness of Devil's Den, but soon I could see them both as they crossed the parking lot and made their way to the car. Ironically, our car was a Ford Escape, and escape they did! But from what? A cat? In no time at all, I knew exactly what it was that had frightened them; it was a strong presence that now swirled around me like a cold autumn wind, and once again I began taking pictures in every direction, certain I would get something on film. But afterward when the film had been developed, the pictures revealed nothing at all. Yet I knew I was in the presence of something dark and angry.

When I got back to the car, Jayne felt the need to explain to me that she wasn't afraid of the cat. "I just felt a sense of panic," she said, "like I had to get out of there as fast as I could."

"I know," I said. "I felt it too!"

I started the engine and put the car in reverse, but as I did, a thought occurred to me. It was some of the most chaotic fighting that took place during the Battle of Gettysburg. I wondered what it was like for the Union soldiers who died there. As the Confederate Army led a hard charge against their position, they must have felt boxed in by the huge boulders that make up Devil's Den. And I'm sure their fear turned to panic as they desperately searched for a way out. Perhaps that was what had frightened my wife; perhaps in some psychic way she was able to feel the fear and panic that had been experienced by others over one hundred years ago.

"Well, what's next?" I asked. "Sachs Bridge?" I looked at the rearview mirror and saw Samantha looking back, her eyes lit up with excitement. "Still wanna walk the bridge?"

"Yeah!"

"Alone in the dark?" I asked.

Samantha smiled broadly. "I'll do it!"

Soon we were turning off the main street onto a narrow dirt road, and at its end Sachs Bridge lay waiting. "There it is," I said, once again looking up at my daughter's reflection in the rearview. But her smile had begun to fade. It was just as I told her it would be; the bridge had become a different place. Where it was once charming and peaceful, it was now dark and isolated. And I knew that like a stone tossed into a pool of calm water, our presence on the bridge would send ripples through time, disturbing the residual energy that until now lay still and quiet.

Sam was quick to get out of the car, but when she began walking toward the bridge, her steps became slow and cautious. Then, looking in each direction, she entered the darkness of Sachs Bridge.

As my daughter's form began to fade into the blackness, I was reminded of that old movie *The Haunting*. There was a scene where the housekeeper, Mrs. Dudly, tried to warn her guests that she doesn't stay after dinner, not after it begins to get dark. "I leave before the darkness comes," she warned, "so there won't be anyone around if you need help! No one could even hear you. No one will come any nearer than town, in the night, in the dark!"

I laughed as the mental image of Mrs. Dudly passed through my mind. "Maybe I should go with her," I said, getting out of the car. But when I caught up with her, she was already halfway across the bridge and didn't seem nearly as frightened as I thought she might be. Together Sam and I walked the rest of the way across Sachs Bridge, and I began taking pictures from its opposite end.

"Where are we supposed to knock?" Sam asked. Uncertain, I suggested we knock in different areas while reciting the words, Virginia, Virginia, Tennessee! Soon Sam and I found ourselves standing in the middle of Sachs Bridge, but nothing was happening, and I was about to suggest we get going when I heard Samantha gasp. Startled, she quickly turned around as though something had happened behind her.

"What's wrong?" I asked. Sam didn't answer at first; she only stared back at the other end of the bridge.

"Nothing," she said. "I just thought I heard something." Sam had become nervous and troubled, and I knew something was bothering her.

"Come on, let's get out of here," I said. As we walked slowly toward the car, I saw her looking over her shoulder, and I was certain something had happened.

"You guys have fun?" Jayne asked as we got back in the car.

"Yeah, it was okay," I said.

Sam remained silent, staring out the window at Sachs Bridge.

After we had gotten well away from the bridge, I looked up at my rearview, and Sam's face wasn't smiling back at me. Instead she sat quietly as though deep in thought. "You okay?"

"I think there was someone else on the bridge," she said. "I heard a man in boots walk up behind me, but when I looked, I didn't see anyone. I could feel him standing there, reaching out as though he wanted to touch me, but there wasn't anyone there. Even when we left, I knew he was still there, standing all alone on the bridge, watching us leave."

After our film had been developed, we found a mysterious cloud formation at the opposite end of the bridge. Could this be a picture of the man who had walked up behind Sam?

CONCLUSION

As an adult, the final hours of darkness have come and gone, leaving the shadow man exposed by the light of day, and I can see clearly now his true nature and cause for being.

Often Hollywood will depict ghosts as ghastly and demonic beings who haunt the living for purposes of vengeance and murder. But our investigations have led us from haunted prisons to abandoned houses where the spirits seem to haunt for some very simple and human reasons. A grieving father relives the death of his beloved son, unseen children laugh and play, and convicts remain behind bars though their lives and sentences ended many years ago. Though at times they were intimidating and even frightening as they watched us trespass across their perceived reality, in each case the spirits we encountered seemed to exist in their own emotionally charged world of memory, a world I one day came to understand.

While passing through my hometown, I took a deliberate detour, a detour that led to my old neighborhood. I drove slowly past the elementary school and then around the block, passing the homes of my childhood friends. I could clearly recall the names and faces of each one and how we laughed, joked, and played together. But as I approached the house where I grew up, I slowed the car to a near stop.

I remembered how I once ran barefoot across the lawn, with my dog chasing close behind. Even the trees were like old friends, reminding me of the days when I climbed them. The house itself was a keepsake of memories. There were birthdays, holidays, and family gatherings, and I wanted nothing more than to step inside where I could see it as it once was.

In my mind, I could envision my mother and father still sitting at the kitchen table, but sadly they're gone now, and my family home belongs to strangers. I never felt such loss, but there was nothing more I could do than drive away and leave the past behind.

Later that evening, I sat back in my chair and tried to imagine what it might be like to haunt. Free from the restrictions of life, there would be no boundaries or locked doors to bar the way, and like a breath of air, I could drift unseen through the world of the living and revisit every moment of the past. The more I thought about it, the more obvious it became: a ghost is nothing more than a spirit retracing the steps he took in life. It even seemed possible that our spirit is comprised of emotional energy and somehow fueled by the memory of life. But what is it that draws their attention to us? Often, people who claim to live in a haunted house will also claim the haunting began during its renovation. Could it be that altering their environment will disrupt the world they remember and awaken them to our physical presence?

Or perhaps there are spirits who haunt for reasons of confusion. If spirits dwell in a world of memory, then travel through both time and space might take place within the limits of thought; that is to say time and distance no longer have meaning. Also, there are many people in the paranormal community who believe the actual moment of death to be a quick and painless transition. If this is true, then a sudden or unexpected death could carry with it the delusion of normalcy. For example, a man is on his way home from work, distracted by his thoughts of home and family. He never sees the car speeding toward him from the left. The collision is abrupt and deadly, his death instantaneous, but is it possible for him to be unaware the accident ever took place?

Thrust suddenly into a world where physical limitations no longer apply, and unaware his commute had been interrupted, he might find himself arriving at home as though nothing were amiss. But for him, time has stopped, and unable to perceive its passing, the illusion may continue for years, decades, or even centuries before he begins to notice that changes are taking place all around him. It's even been suggested that a spirit lost in such a state of confusion might come to believe that he himself is the one being haunted. Objects are unexplainably moved, disembodied voices echo throughout the house, while the vague image of a stranger is glimpsed from the corner of his eye. At some point, the spirit might try making contact with the ghostly intruders who torment him, but eventually he will come to understand the situation and move on to whatever world awaits him.

On the other hand, there may be those who simply refuse to accept their demise, and in some cases that level of denial can be even deeper. In life, we frequently ignore the truth, blaming others for our own misdeeds and shortcomings. We simply refuse to see or hear anything we aren't willing to accept, turning reality itself into a comfortable lie. For them, death is the only avenue by which it's possible to face the truth and untangle the confusion between fantasy and reality.

Another type of spirit Jayne and I have encountered is what I like to call a free spirit. Unlike other spirits who seem to be retracing the steps they took in life, a free spirit isn't confined to any particular area and on occasion will follow the living. When Jayne and I first began our investigations, our home was as common as any other. Now, however, doors can be heard to open and then slam shut, lights turn themselves on and off, and the faint scent of roses lingers in the air while footsteps are heard climbing the stairs. On one occasion, I had been watching television when the fifty-three-inch screen grew dark, reflecting the room at a wide angle. In that reflection, I could see the apparition of a boy standing in the corner. Suddenly the scene changed, and the screen once again lit up. The reflection I had seen disappeared, leaving no trace of the young intruder. Afterward, a thorough search of the house revealed nothing. I was alone! At times, each family member has caught a glimpse of a man who sits at the top of the stairs, an old woman, and the boy, but have they been there all along? Or did they follow us home from any one of the many locations we've investigated? In either case, it seems the deeper we delve into their world, the more interest they have in ours.

In some cases, it would seem obvious that spirits are able to see, hear, and communicate with the living. But in the case of residual hauntings, the spirits involved seem completely unaware of our living presence. Though this phenomenon is commonly associated with spirit activity, there may in fact be no ghost at all. During times of great stress or tragedy, emotional energy can be imprinted on the atmosphere with enough force to leave a lasting impression. This phenomenon, also referred to as place memory, is something like a video tape playing past events, but when witnessed it can sometimes be mistaken for a haunting.

I myself had an experience with place memory, but for me the event was rather unique. I had come home from work one evening, and soon after, a loud quarrel erupted between my son and daughter. Annoyed by the commotion, I got up and headed for the foot of the stairs, but suddenly the sounds of a fight turned to laughter. Still annoyed by the disturbance, I decided to flip the lights on and off a few times to get their attention and ask them to keep it down. But as I reached for the switch, the sound suddenly stopped, and I froze in my tracks when I remembered that my wife had gone shopping, and the kids went with her!

Although my experience with place memory might seem harmless, for others the event is much more sinister. Residual hauntings often reflect acts of violence and murder, and if the environment is heavily stained by this kind of energy and can be felt or perceived by the living, then it might also affect a person's emotional state of mind. Likewise, a ghost, which I believe to be comprised primarily of emotional energy, might also influence a person's thinking. Spirits reliving a turbulent past will generate negative energy, and anyone sensitive enough to perceive their suffering might be vulnerable to its effect. A once emotionally stable person might become irrational, suffering from feelings of jealousy, anger, even thoughts of suicide or violence.

Hollywood will solve the problem with an exorcism, or perhaps a white witch will utter a few magic words that will send the evil spirit packing. But in reality, it may not be so easy to force a ghost out of the house. After all, it isn't possible to physically eject a nonphysical entity, and I have little faith in candles or incantations. Even in the movies, people who have had an exorcism done will sometimes complain that paranormal activity has worsened or become hostile in nature. And why wouldn't it? Think of the arrogance it would take to order someone "in the name of God" to leave their own home. And why would any spirit who believes he himself to be the rightful owner of the house be so compliant? However, if the spirit is aware of your living presence, then perhaps he's only trying to make contact, but in his confused state he has become like a drunken man, disoriented, irrational, even frightening in his efforts to communicate.

For some, these events are nothing more than a passing curiosity, but for others, the effects of a haunting can be overwhelming, and the only solution is to relocate.

Certainly the spirit world is a reality, and evidence of it can be found in all walks of life. From city to city and throughout the countryside, stories of the paranormal abound. Yet skeptics persist in their efforts to prove that ghosts don't exist. A frequent attempt at debunking the paranormal is to say that most of the pictures we offer as evidence are nothing more than common mistakes in photography, and I'd like to emphasize the word *most*. Orbs, for example, are a favorite of debunkers. In their opinion, all orbs are nothing more than dust on the camera lens, and I must admit, dust can be a problem when using digital equipment. However, it can be easily identified; dust is perfectly round with a rim surrounding its outer edge, and the center will be textured. It might even reveal what will appear to be a smiling face. But actual orbs are often solid white, or translucent and misshapen with no rim around the outer edge. They might also show up as a swirling cloud of white mist or a drifting point of light. In order to avoid the problems created by dust, I only use a standard film loaded camera and 400 film, yet I still get orbs! Skeptics will then explain that a few drops of water during the developing process can also cause orb-like images to appear. Whatever the problem might be, I've seen and taken hundreds of pictures, but orbs seem to show up only in the ones taken at haunted locations.

Another attempt at debunking the paranormal is to recreate the evidence provided by ghost hunters. The idea is simple; if they can recreate it, then it must be a hoax. But that only proves they have an ability to falsify evidence. Remember, it's also possible to counterfeit money, and if you go by their logic, your savings account is worthless. Once again, their attempts at disproving the existence of ghosts have fallen short, and though their efforts are tireless, they might also be in vain.

Eyewitness accounts of the paranormal continue, and they come from all walks of life, from societies most revered to trusted family members. Yet many of us still view the paranormal with disbelief. Skepticism is, however, a necessary part of any investigation. Without some measure of disbelief, anyone might find himself jumping at shadows or looking foolish when the true cause of the haunting is discovered. During any investigation, the first rule should always be to look for a logical explanation. If no such explanation can be found, then and only then can the paranormal be considered a possibility.

I have the same measure of skepticism for anyone who claims to have psychic abilities. After all, anyone can say they see or sense a presence while the rest of us stand by unable to dispute the validity of their claims. Psychics also describe the brilliant white light of God and how they guide lost souls to their salvation. But is it possible for anyone to see into the next world and understand it more clearly than the spirits who dwell there? Perhaps one day we'll accept the next world without question, and schools will teach our children the facts of life and death. Such spiritual enlightenment could lead mankind further down the road of evolution, softening even the hardest of hearts as we begin to realize the true value of life. But for now, there is no proof that ghosts exist, and no one knows what happens to us when we die. But in these final hours of darkness, I have come to believe that ghosts and spirits are real, and if this is true, then there is most certainly a spirit realm. But this is a world yet to be explored, and no one knows what else might be watching us from a reality that exists beyond the reach of our five senses.

Seasons don't fear the reaper, nor do the wind, the sun and the rain, and we can be like they are. Come on baby take my hand, we'll be able to fly!

—Blue Oyster Cult

ABOUT THE BOOK

Follow the author on an in-depth investigation of the paranormal that will lead you through the darkened corridors of a haunted insane asylum, said to have been the sight of satanic rituals, and two abandoned prisons, both which house not only the murderous souls of the convicts who were once incarcerated there but also the place memory of their evil deeds.

In this true account of a paranormal investigation, you will visit many other locations that are said to be haunted and discover the truth behind the shadow man who turned the author's childhood dreams into nightmares.

Printed in the United States
By Bookmasters